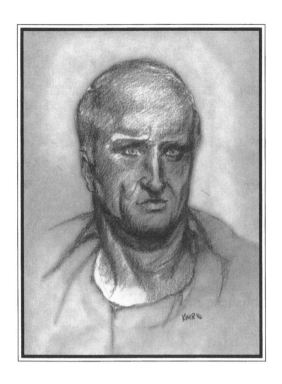

CICERO'S FIRST CATILINARIAN ORATION

with Introduction,
Running Vocabularies, and Notes

by Karl Frerichs

with a Foreword by
Robert W. Cape, Jr.

BOLCHAZY-CARDUCCI Publishers, Inc.
Wauconda, Illinois

General Editor:
Laurie Haight Keenan

Cover illustration:
Portrait of Cicero
Kay McGinnis Ritter

Cover design:
Kay McGinnis Ritter

Bolchazy-Carducci Publishers, Inc.
1570 Baskin Road
Mundelein, Illinois 60060

http://www.bolchazy.com

Printed in the United States of America
by United Graphics

2015

ISBN 978-0-86516-341-6

———————————————————

Library of Congress Cataloging-in-Publication Data

Cicero, Marcus Tullius.
    [In Catilinam. Oratio I]
    Cicero's first Catilinarian oration / with introduction, running
vocabularies, and notes by Karl Frerichs.
        p.   cm.
    Oration in Latin, introduction and notes in English.
    Includes bibliographical references (p.).
    ISBN 0-86516-341-3 (pap. : alk. paper)
    1. Rome--History--Conspiracy of Catiline, 65-62 B.C. 2. Speeches,
addresses, etc., Latin. I. Frerichs, Karl, 1962-   . II. Title.
PA6279.C31 1997
937'.05--DC21   96-49454
                                                              CIP

Contents

Foreword v

Preface vi

Introduction For Students vii

Historical Introduction

    Cicero and His Ascent to Power viii

    Catiline and Conspiracy ix

    Cicero after the Conspiracy xii

    Roman Oratory xiv

Glossary of Terms and Figures of Speech xvi

In L. Catilinam Oratio Prima

    Vocabulary, Notes and Text 1

Table of Abbreviations 50

Table of First Name Abbreviations 50

Vocabulary 51

Bibliography 62

FOREWORD

"O tempora, o mores!" What Latin student has not heard these words? And today, more and more students are learning — and saying! — them. This is good news. Not because our times are so bad (I leave that for others to decide), but because it means more students are again reading Cicero.

Interest in Cicero is growing. Scholarly studies of the orations, letters, and philosophical works are enhancing our appreciation of Cicero's contribution to his contemporary political and intellectual milieu.* A new guide to teaching his works and several new school editions of the important writings are making Cicero's Latin more accessible to the modern high school teacher and student. (See Hayes and Lawall, 1995, and other items in the *Bibliography*.) This follows a long period in which it was fashionable to disparage Cicero and the study of his works. As a result, many teachers who now wish to teach Cicero's speeches, letters, or philosophical essays may not have read them. With the increasing interest in enhancing Latin pedagogy, the new materials are providing a wealth of information for teachers at all levels.

Karl Frerichs's new commentary on Cicero's *First Catilinarian Oration* is an important contribution to

the growing list of Ciceroniana. Students can now read the whole speech with the essential vocabulary and grammar assistance they need. The format of the information on the page makes it more comfortable to read and review the Latin text. A historical narrative introduces the oration, and complicated details of fact and interpretation do not obtrude or overwhelm the first-time reader. The text is suitable for those who are teaching Cicero for the first time as well the seasoned Ciceronian pedagogue.

As oratory returns to the Latin classroom, it is important that the *First Catilinarian* receives a commentary designed for the modern student. Students who read this speech become members of an enormous fellowship of readers from Cicero's own day to the present. For centuries students have memorized the now immortal opening lines, "Quo usque tandem abutere, Catilina, patientia nostra?...," and declaimed them among Roman ruins, at school reunions, and at posh dinner parties. They have been parodied in literature and engraved on a rhetoric teacher's funeral monument. They live beside the other two immortalized opening lines of ancient Roman works: "Gallia est omnis divisa in partes tres...," and "Arma virumque cano, Troiae qui primus ab oris...." With Frerichs's edition, the whole of Cicero's *First Catilinarian* can again be taught early in the curriculum, and passed on to another generation of readers.

Robert W. Cape, Jr.
Austin College
Sherman, Texas

---

* For a convenient bibliography available on the World Wide Web, visit the following site: http://www.dla.utexas.edu/depts/classics/documents/Cic.html.

PREFACE

In preparing this reader, I have consulted many other commentaries on the *Catilinarians*, but I have especially benefited from the notes by Moore and Barse and by Kelsey and Meinecke. Whenever possible, I have presented fresh suggestions for translation, but in many cases I have followed the suggestions offered by previous commentators. For the historical introduction, I am especially indebted to MacDonald's introduction in the Loeb edition, which provides an excellent overview of the political events surrounding this speech. The other resources that I found helpful are listed in the *Bibliography*. Those intimately familiar with the scholarship will see the influence of these resources scattered throughout the text, but, given the nature of this work, I do not list each reference. For the most part, I followed the text of A. C. Clark's *Oxford Classical Text*. I have departed from Clark's edition most significantly by inserting more paragraph divisions. All other departures are limited to regularization of archaic spellings and punctuation. Each departure was made with a view to making the Latin more accessible to the intermediate student.

The encouragement and criticism of many people have strengthened this reader immeasurably. Dr. Henry Strater used an early version in his own classes, and his insights provided an essential balance to my own methods. Pat Aliazzi helped on numerous points of research. John Gladstone edited an early draft with a tenacity and thoroughness that stand as a model for me. The students in my Latin III course in the spring of 1996 — Rodney Russell, in particular — spent many hours proofing the vocabulary sections for inconsistencies in presentation. Additionally, Dr. Robert Cape's assistance with the manuscript brought a scholarly balance to the historical issues. His comments forced me to reconsider many of my assumptions and saved me from several errors of fact. Kay McGinnis Ritter always provided good advice on layout, computer problems and graphics. Laurie Haight and Ladislaus Bolchazy gave timely advice and support on all manner of publication difficulties. Any oversights and errors must, of course, remain solely my own.

Finally, I thank University School for support in the form of summer grants. To Marin Ritter, Jenny Hastings, Paul Aucoin, and my parents, goes an appreciation deeper than can be properly expressed here.

INTRODUCTION FOR STUDENTS

This book's primary purpose is to help make sense of Cicero's Latin without the constant aid of a teacher or a translation. The most important point to remember — and the easiest to forget — is that Cicero meant to be understood. Accordingly, always try to understand Cicero's point. Be sure to bring your knowledge of the political context, setting, and history to bear on the meaning of each section. Although a particular sentence's point may not be obvious, always practice the same process.

First, read the entire assigned passage aloud. Do this a couple of times, attempting to get a feel for where the word groups begin and end. During the second reading, try to anticipate what Cicero's point is, based upon the recognizable vocabulary and syntax; quickly attempt to infer the meaning of the words, and try to make an educated guess at the overall meaning.

Next, for the **first** time, use the vocabulary on the page facing the text to verify the meaning of words, or to learn the meaning of unfamiliar words. These vocabularies, which are in alphabetical order for quick reference, provide unfamiliar words or reinforce the more common ones. Now revise your original translation in light of this new information. Working on one sentence at a time, be sure to translate each specific word, or indicate which words you don't understand. Finally, use the commentary below the line on each page. These notes often contain hints on translation and structure, or they give more background information. Now try to work out a complete translation of each sentence, always with a view to its meaning.

A final note on the system of references in this book is in order. All Arabic numbers in the notes refer to the line numbers to the right of the Latin text. In the Latin text itself, however, two types of bracketed numbers appear: the Roman numerals, e.g. [IV], indicate the thirteen traditional "chapter" divisions of the speech; the Arabic numbers, e.g. [4], indicate the more recent paragraph divisions, which modern scholars use when citing sections of the speech. Additionally, most of the name abbreviations in the Latin text are explained in the notes, but all of them appear in the *Table of First Name Abreviations* on page 50 and in the complete vocabulary at the end of the book. All symbols and abbreviations are defined in the *Table of Abbreviations* on page 50. Important terms in the notes and *Historical Introduction* appear in boldface type and are usually explained the first time they appear. All such terms may be found in the *Glossary of Terms and Figures of Speech* on pages xvi through xviii.

HISTORICAL INTRODUCTION

Cicero and His Ascent to Power

Marcus Tullius Cicero was born to an **equestrian** family in 106 B.C. near Arpinum, a town approximately 60 miles southeast of Rome. Since Arpinum's citizens had only received Roman citizenship in 188 B.C., any of her citizens seeking a political career at Rome faced the difficulties of an outsider. Arpinum had, however, produced the famous general Gaius Marius who held the consulship at Rome seven times; thus Cicero had the advantage of a local precedent for political success. In order to insure the best chance of a public career at Rome, Cicero's father saw to it that his gifted son received most of his education there. Cicero assumed the **toga virilis** in 91 B.C., and was apprenticed to Quintus Mucius Scaevola, the leading public speaker of the time. Cicero now spent most of his time observing the political and judicial orations at the **Forum**. In 89 B.C., Cicero served under Pompey the Great's father in the Social War (90-88 B.C.), but emerged with no taste for military service. During the conflict between Marius and Sulla, Cicero continued studying rhetoric, and he avoided any serious entanglements between the competing factions. In 80 B.C., at the age of 26, Cicero delivered his first criminal speech in defense of Roscius, who was accused of murder by supporters of Sulla. This case was a bold choice for a novice speaker, because Sulla had recently carried out the bloody proscription of all of his political enemies. Cicero was successful in his defense, but the stress of his copious preparation of this and subsequent briefs left him physically exhausted. With the hope of honing his rhetorical skills and restoring his physical health, Cicero set out for Greece in 79 B.C. After studying with the leading Greek rhetoricians in Athens and Asia Minor, Cicero returned to Rome in 77 B.C. and sometime shortly thereafter married Terentia.

Cicero was now ready to begin his political career in earnest. His steady rise through the **cursus honorum**, the sequence of offices, would be all the more remarkable because of his status as a **novus homo**: He did not have any consuls among his ancestors. In 76 B.C., at the age of 31, he was elected **quaestor**, the first step in the **cursus honorum**. In 75 B.C., he proceeded to administer the finances of Sicily with fairness and restraint. The Sicilians remained grateful for that fairness. As a result of their

trust, in 71 B.C. the Sicilians asked Cicero to prosecute Verres, the **propraetor** of Sicily from 73-71 B.C. In spite of Verres's extensive bribery of the judges, Cicero managed to bring the case to trial. Cicero faced a second challenge in that Verres had retained Hortensius, the leading lawyer in Rome. Cicero's copious research and bold trial tactics, however, forced Verres to flee Rome after Cicero's opening speech on the first day of the trial. Cicero carried off a huge victory both for the Sicilians and for his own standing at the bar. He later published a total of seven speeches which he had prepared for the case. Because of his energetic research and rhetorical polish, Cicero's reputation in the courts now surpassed even Hortensius's.

In 69 B.C., Cicero climbed the next step in the **cursus honorum** by serving as **aedile**. Although officially an optional office, most rising politicians preferred to hold it to exploit the opportunities it provided to curry favor with the public. Instead of the expensive gladiatorial games **aediles** often gave, Cicero sponsored the public production of Greek plays and provided the people with cheap meat from Sicily. In 66 B.C., his efforts in the courts and as **aedile** paid off: he was elected **praetor** at the top of the polls. In the same year, he delivered his first speech at a public meeting, a **contio**, in support of expanding Pompey's command in the Mediterranean to include the war against Mithridates. Thus Cicero was perceived as aligned with Pompey against Crassus in spite of the fact that Pompey's support for Cicero would always be moderate at best.

In 65 B.C., Cicero began campaigning for his election to the consulship. The elections were held in the summer of 64 B.C.; and once again Cicero came in at the top of the poll, with Gaius Antonius Hybrida, the uncle of Marc Antony, as the second **consul**. Lucius Sergius Catilina came in third. Since competition for the consulship had increased, it was very difficult for the young **nobiles** to hold office at the youngest age allowed by law, or **suo anno**. Cicero's election **suo anno** and his status as a **novus homo** threatened the members of the old families who saw election as their birthright. Thus, what Cicero counted as his greatest success, Catiline, the **nobilis**, saw as personal setback. Cicero would have to deal with the results of Catiline's mounting disappointment throughout his consulship.

Catiline and Conspiracy

Catiline, born of an old noble family, initially had many supporters among the **patricians**. He had risen through the steps of the **cursus honorum** without interruption; but, when he returned in 66 B.C. from his propraetorship in Africa, African ambassadors had already arrived in Rome to protest his misrule. In spite of the allegations, Catiline decided to run for the consulship. Catiline's candidacy was further complicated by the fact that he was attempting to run in what was to be the second consular election of that summer. The winners of the first election had been successfully prosecuted on charges of bribery. Catiline's candidacy in the second election was disallowed supposedly because he had not stood in the original election, but early sources are not absolutely clear on the reasons for his disqualification. By his early and legally tenuous attempt to stand for the consulship, Catiline did reveal a certain disregard for both the judicial and electoral processes at Rome. This disregard would characterize his actions for the next three and a half years.

In 65 B.C., Catiline could not stand for election because he was still on trial for his misrule in Africa. Although he was eventually acquitted, Catiline's second chance to stand for the consulship had passed. Finally, in 64 B.C., Catiline stood for the consulship against Cicero, Antonius, and others. After a campaign of mudslinging, Catiline's and Antonius's support from the **optimates**, the aristocratic party, waned. The phenomenally wealthy Crassus dropped all his backing; Caesar, who would rely heavily on Crassus and other wealthy Romans in his bid for **pontifex maximus** in 63 B.C., no longer supported Catiline in spite of his **patrician** family. Thus, Cicero defeated men who had prominent political ties and family names. This rebuff further insulted Catiline's **nobilitas**.

In 63 B.C., the year of Cicero and Antonius's consulship, Catiline was forced to turn to less reputable citizens in his attempts to secure support for his election. Appealing to the financially distressed through his support for **novae tabellae**, or a cancellation of debts, he managed to alienate even further the support of the **optimates**. At the elections themselves,

Cesare Maccari (1840-1919), "Cicero Accuses Catiline." This is the most famous painting of Cicero's consulship. Maccari vividly depicts the estrangement of Catiline from his fellow senators described in lines 152-158. The painting, however, has some interesting historical problems: It depicts the meeting in the Curia (Senate house) rather than in the Temple of Jupiter Stator, and there were not permanent seats in the Curia. Also note the improbability of Cicero's hair being gray at the age of 43, while Catiline, who was older than Cicero, looks much younger.

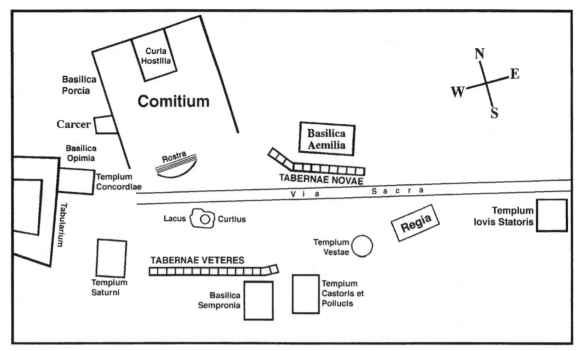

The Roman Forum in the Time of Cicero

Cicero felt enough of a threat from Catiline's behavior that he dressed in a breastplate and was accompanied by an armed bodyguard. Catiline was again defeated. Having already garnered some support from the politically and financially dispossessed, he now began his preparations for revolution in earnest.

Catiline openly paraded himself in front of the sons of the men proscribed by Sulla, and nine men would eventually emerge as his chief organizers in Rome. Among these, Publius Cornelius Lentulus Sura, Gaius Cornelius Cethegus, Lucius Statilius, Publius Gabinius Capito, and Marcus Caeparius eventually emerged as the most brash and foolhardy. In Etruria, Gaius Manlius was enrolling men for his army. On October 19, Cicero called a meeting of the Senate to present vague evidence that Manlius was preparing an open insurrection at Faesulae, a town in northwest Etruria. That day or the following, Quintus Arrius brought specific information on the legion being equipped in Etruria and the plans for a **coup d'état**. Catiline himself, however, had been careful to avoid any traceable connection to that army in order to continue his operations in Rome. With the new information from Arrius, on October 21, the Senate became

alarmed and passed the **senatus consultum ultimum**. This vague decree encouraged the consul to take any action necessary to stave off a threat to the state. Catiline now saw that his position in Rome was weakening. After aborting plans to have Manlius bring his troops closer to Rome, Catiline called a meeting on the evening of November 6 to parcel out commands throughout Rome and the southern districts of Italy. Catiline also arranged for Cicero to be murdered the next morning. Since Cicero by now had a good network of informers, he turned back the would-be murderers the next day, November 7. On November 8, Cicero called a meeting of the Senate at the temple of Jupiter Stator, since that building was easier to defend than the **Curia**.

Cicero may have assumed, because Catiline had failed to destabilize Rome from within, that Catiline would depart for Etruria before the meeting. Cicero, then, could use that departure as strong evidence of Catiline's part in the revolution. In a direct challenge to Cicero's authority, Catiline came to the meeting since he knew that Cicero in fact had no concrete evidence. Cicero then delivered a speech that surely must have had many improvised elements, given the unexpected presence of Catiline. Later known as the *First Catilinarian Oration*, this speech still stands as a masterpiece of invective. The difficulty of Cicero's position, however, is clearly revealed: It was one thing for the Senate to disapprove of Catiline's actions, but quite another to condemn a fellow **nobilis** without evidence. It is important in reading the speech to note both Cicero's rhetorical polish and his caution. As for Catiline, sources differ on his reaction to the speech: Either he left the Senate without word, or he denied any knowledge of a conspiracy — playing on the audience's possible sympathy. Whatever his immediate reaction, he departed from Rome that night to join Manlius at Faesulae.

The following day, November 9, Cicero delivered before the people the *Second Catilinarian Oration* to inform them of the events in the Senate the day before. Around the middle of November, Catiline had reached Faesulae; he and Manlius were now in open revolt, and the Senate declared both men **hostes**, enemies of the state. At the beginning of December, envoys from the Allobroges, a Gallic tribe, were approached by the conspirators and asked for their sup-

port since their northern position would protect the rear of Catiline's army. The Allobroges immediately went to their tribe's hereditary Roman patron, Quintus Fabius Sanga, and asked for advice. After consulting with Cicero, Sanga instructed the envoys to play along with the conspirators and to ask the conspirators for written and sealed descriptions of the conspiracy. With amazing naiveté, the conspirators agreed to supply the envoys with the letters. Early in the morning of December 3, the Allobroges and Titus Volturcius, who quickly turned state's evidence, were arrested as they crossed the Mulvian bridge about two miles north of Rome. (This bridge — also known as the Milvian bridge — was also the site of Constantine's great victory in A.D. 312.) The envoys of the Allobroges, after feigning resistance and handing over documents obtained from the conspirators, were released. Additionally, Cicero ordered Cethegus's house to be searched, and a cache of arms was found. The five chief conspirators who could be linked to the conspiracy through the letters or eyewitnesses were ordered to be arrested. Cicero then called a meeting of the Senate, wherein the letters to the Allobroges were

Alinari/Art Resource, NY

Via Sacra. *This view of the Forum looks to the southeast along the* **Via Sacra**. *The* **rostra** *and* **comitium** *are to the left.*

read and the conspirators confessed. Afterward, he came before the people in the **Forum** and delivered the *Third Catilinarian Oration*, in which he detailed the proceedings. The Senate met again on the next day and declared that the conspirators had acted **contra rem publicam**.

On December 5, Cicero called another meeting of the Senate to decide the handling of the five conspirators arrested at Rome. Most senators spoke for immediate execution without trial, but Caesar, adopting what would become his trademark **popularis** stance, rose in opposition to this unconstitutional action. Seeing that a majority favored summary punishment, Cicero interrupted the debate and in the *Fourth Catilinarian Oration* carefully redirected the argument towards support for the death penalty. Cato, the archconservative who already that year had proved himself zealous in the enforcement of bribery laws, rose in support of the decisive action. The Senate agreed: Lentulus, Cethegus, and the three others were immediately taken to the **Tullianum** and choked to death while the crowd waited outside to hear word of the executions. As a result of his energy and dedication to the Republic, Cicero was hailed **pater patriae.**

Cicero's support was not universal, however. On December 10, Quintus Caecilius Metellus Nepos was elected **tribune of the plebs**; he later declared that anyone who has executed a Roman citizen without trial should not be allowed to speak before the people. Accordingly, Nepos did not allow Cicero to give the final oration traditionally delivered on a consul's last day of office. In order to undercut Nepos's **de facto** gag order, in his departing oath Cicero swore that he alone had saved the Republic. On January 3 of 62 B.C., the Senate passed a resolution indemnifying all those who had acted against the conspirators. Nepos, frustrated by the action, immediately left Rome in protest, and Caesar, after being duly chastised, stayed quietly in Rome. Outside of Rome, Antonius pursued Catiline's one legion until its defeat near Pistoria in mid-January of 62 B.C. Thus the conspiracy was stopped without posing any real threat to the state.

Cicero after the Conspiracy

In spite of the Senate's decree, Cicero would soon find himself vulnerable to the vicissitudes of Roman politics. In 62 B.C., Clodius, an erstwhile member of the nobility, was caught at the rites of the **Bona Dea** being held at Julius Caesar's house. Men were strictly forbidden from these rites, and accordingly Clodius was brought to trial. He claimed that he had not even been in Rome at the time, but Cicero rose to say that he had seen Clodius in Rome just hours before the ceremony. By destroying Clodius's alibi, Cicero had acquired a bitter personal enemy. Over the next few years, Cicero also found himself opposing the interests of Rome's most powerful men. In 60 B.C., Caesar, Pompey, and Crassus formed the so-called First Triumvirate, which in fact was only an informal agreement that none of them would take any major actions without first consulting the other two. Cicero spoke publicly against this alliance. Thus, in 59 B.C., the **consul** Caesar allowed Clodius to be adopted into a **plebeian** family, and accordingly Clodius could be elected to the office of **tribune of the plebs**. When he became tribune, his first action was to exile anyone who had put a citizen to death without trial. The initial proclamation, although it did not name Cicero, was clearly directed at him for his actions in 63 B.C. Soon, however, Clodius had another resolution passed that specifically named Cicero. Although he delayed as long as he could, Cicero was forced to leave Italy by March of 58 B.C. After his departure, his house on the **Palatine** was burned by Clodius's mob.

By 57 B.C., as the other triumvirs were getting disgusted with Clodius's wretched excesses, Cicero regained some favor among the triumvirs. Pompey then became an open supporter of Cicero's return. As soon as the decree for his recall was passed by the Senate, Cicero crossed over from Greece to Brundisium and made his trip back to Rome at a leisurely pace. He was greeted by cheers in all the towns along the Appian Way.

During the 50s B.C., Caesar was in Gaul, while Crassus attempted a military campaign against the Parthians. Crassus was defeated and killed at Carrhae in Mesopotamia, and accordingly the political setting at Rome was now dominated by Pompey. In 51 B.C., Cicero finally accepted a proconsulship in Cilicia in Asia Minor and departed for that province in July. He governed fairly, if not with any major distinction, in spite of resolving some minor border skirmishes. When he returned to Rome in 49 B.C., civil war was imminent. He tried to negotiate a compromise between Pompey and Caesar, but to no avail. Eventually, after hesitating a great deal, he followed Pompey to Greece where Pompey was defeated at Pharsalus in August of 48 B.C. After a pardon by Caesar, Cicero retired from

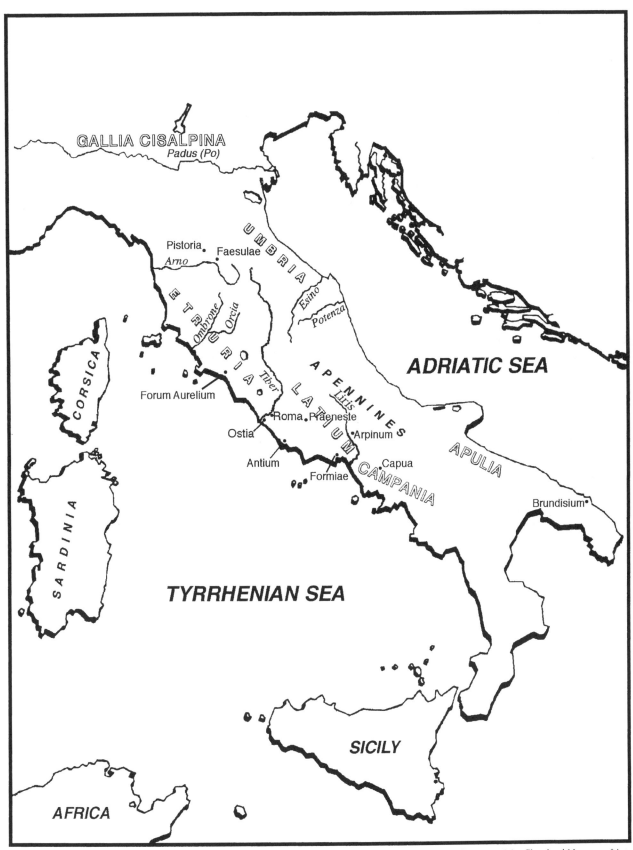

GALLIA CISALPINA
Padus (Po)

Pistoria
Arno Faesulae

UMBRIA

E
T
R
U
R
I
A

Ombrone *Orcia*

Esino

Potenza

Forum Aurelium

Tiber

A
P
E
N
N
I
N
E
S

ADRIATIC SEA

L
A
T
I
U
M

Liris

Roma Praeneste
•Arpinum

Ostia

Antium

Formiae

CAMPANIA

Capua

APULIA

Brundisium•

CORSICA

SARDINIA

TYRRHENIAN SEA

SICILY

AFRICA

Italy

public life and spent his time on the writing of philosophy. In 46 B.C., Cicero divorced Terentia and married Publilia, a wealthy girl for whom he had been guardian. Early in 45 B.C., Cicero's daughter, Tullia, died. This loss sent him into depression and the further writing of philosophy. After Publilia did not show proper grief over the loss of Tullia, Cicero divorced her as well.

In 44 B.C., after Caesar's assassination, Cicero made his final ascent to political influence. Hoping to reconcile himself with Antony, he returned to Rome, but Antony rebuffed him. In August he began a series of speeches known as the *Philippics* since they resembled in characterization and invective the speeches of Demosthenes against Philip of Macedon. The fourteen surviving speeches are harshly critical of Antony's personal and public character. Antony and his wife Fulvia took deep offense. In 43 B.C., Octavian, Antony and Lepidus acquired from the Senate absolute authority as a triumvirate "to restore the Republic." They took this opportunity to exact revenge on individuals and issued a proscription list, as Sulla had done. Cicero's name was one of the first on that list. Cicero fled Rome; but, after his ship was blown back by winds at Caieta near Formiae, he retreated to his villa at Formiae where Antony's men caught up with him. In spite of a last-minute effort to escape, Cicero finally offered his head to his murderers. At Antony's order, Marcus Tullius Cicero was murdered on December 7, 43 B.C.: his head and hands were then cut off and nailed to the **rostra** in the **Forum**.

Roman Oratory

Roman oratory challenges us with an aspect of culture that is surprisingly different from our own. Today, since speech-making is only one small part of a larger image presented through the media, a public figure often seeks not to make mistakes rather than to project a strong, intelligent persona. For Romans, however, oratory was central to their effectiveness as public leaders, since oratory's primary purpose was to persuade an audience to approve of the speaker's point of view. Even Romans who were most famous as generals were often evaluated on their ability to speak persuasively. Therefore, Romans paid careful attention to oratorical practice from early in their history.

In the middle of the second century B.C., Greek models for developing speaking skills started gaining acceptance, and affluent Romans traveled to Athens and Rhodes to study **rhetoric**. The earliest treatise that still survives, the *Rhetorica ad Herennium*, dates from the 80s B.C. and roughly coincides with Cicero's own education in rhetoric. Following Greek rhetoric closely, it gives the three broad categories of speaking as judicial (legal speeches), deliberative (speeches advocating a course of action), and demonstrative (speeches of praise or blame). Further, it prescribes that a student know the theory of speech composition, imitate models, and practice exercises. Within the theory of speech composition, there are five parts of speech development: invention (roughly equivalent to research), arrangement, style, memory, and delivery (*Rhetorica ad Herennium* I.ii.3). Throughout the educational process, students were exhorted to practice exercises in memory and delivery. Additionally, an older Roman adolescent frequently visited the **Forum** to hear speeches in the courts.

When the young citizen matured, his formal education ended. Now he would hope to have a chance to begin his speaking career either in the courts or as a minor speaker before the Senate. The courts in the **Forum** conducted business nearly every non-festival day. For a **novus homo** of Cicero's disposition, the prominence gained from judicial oratory was an essential tool for his political ambition, because it provided a chance to curry favor with the prominent families of Rome. A second venue for speaking was the **contio**, or a political speech before the general citizenry. A **contio** was delivered before an assembly (**comitia**) in explanation of senatorial legislation, or to rally the support of the people on a particular issue. As a Roman rose in prominence and political connections, he could expect more opportunities to speak at **contiones**. Finally, oratory directly influenced the debates in the Senate, and a man's influence could be seen from his prominence in senatorial debates. The most influential men were allowed to speak earlier in senatorial debates; that is, the most prestigous man would be asked to state his opinion to the Senate first. Strong speaking skills only bolstered one's influence in these debates.

Since oratory had such a prominent position in the political process, the Romans needed to pay attention to the many details that would create an effective speech. Among these was the formal organization of a speech. Although the divisions vary, the *Rhetorica ad Herennium* (I.iii.4) gives the following six parts of a judicial speech: the **exordium**, the introduction; the **narratio**, in which the speaker gives the facts; the **propositio**, a statement of what is agreed upon and what is contested; the **confirmatio**, a presentation of the proofs in support of the case; the **refutatio**, which argues against the opponent's points; and the **peroratio**, the conclusion, which often makes a strong emotional appeal to the audience. Although speakers tried to adhere to this pattern, individual situations often demanded the omission of one or more sections. Since the *First Catilinarian Oration* was delivered before the Senate, the text does not strictly follow the prescribed judicial organization — the speech, in fact, defies such a pat analysis. Cicero does, however, use many of the argumentative techniques common to the formal sections of a judicial speech.

In addition to organization, a Roman speaker crafted his language to match his particular purpose and audience. **Style** — the elements that combine to make a speaker's language distinctive — emerges from many different verbal techniques, or figures. Quintilian, the first century A.D. rhetorician, defines a figure as "any form of speech changed by skill" (*Institutio Oratoria* IX.i.14). In other words, any intentional deviation from everyday language could be considered a figure. This broad definition, unfortunately, does little to limit exactly what a figure is. In fact, rhetoricians in the classical and Renaissance periods identified over 200 different figures. While simply memorizing vast lists of figures will do little to help us understand Cicero, an understanding of the most common figures will deepen our appreciation of his oratorical skill. The following glossary contains some of the many figures commonly used by Cicero.

Marcus Tullius Cicero

GLOSSARY OF TERMS AND FIGURES OF SPEECH

Figures of Speech are indicated by italics and are followed by line number(s) of a prominent example in the text.

Aedile: The second office in the **cursus honorum**; responsibilities: public works projects, organizing and paying for the public games.

Alliteration: The repetition of a consonant sound, usually at the beginning of successive words. (100)

Allusion: A brief reference to information with which the author assumes the audience is familiar, but which is outside the context of a work. The goal of such a reference is to bring to the audience a deeper understanding or appreciation. (21)

Amicitia: An informal, long-standing alliance between patrons who regarded the standing and interests of their "friends" before making any political decisions.

Analogy: An extended form of simile which compares two categorically dissimilar items, ideas or objects in order to explain the less familiar in terms of the more familiar. (296-299)

Anaphora: The repetition of the same word(s) at the beginning of successive clauses or phrases. (6-8)

Antithesis: A rhetorical balancing of opposite ideas or phrases for a sense of emphasis or contrast. (38-39)

Asyndeton: The omission of customary connecting words to create a "rapid-fire" effect. (86-89)

Bona Dea: A Roman religious ceremony attended only by the women of Rome. Not too much is known of the proceedings, except that Clodius, disguised as a woman, interrupted the ceremony in 62 B.C.

Campus Martius: The field just to the north and west of the **Pomerium** in the flood plain of the Tiber. The Romans originally used it to marshal troops, but later it was used primarily as assembly point for the **comitia centuriata**.

Censor: The highest political office in Rome, which gave the holders sweeping powers. Two were elected at five year intervals for an eighteen month term; responsibilities: expelling from the Senate members who no longer meet the property or moral qualifications, administering the census of citizens, and the letting of public works projects.

Chiasmus: A "crossing over." An ABBA or ABCBA, etc., arrangement of elements in a line. (62)

Climax: The highpoint of an argument following a **crescendo**. (211)

Comitia: The assemblies of the people called by groups. The most common in Cicero's time were the **comitia tributa** which distributed all citizens into 35 tribes; and the **comitia centuriata** which divided the citizenry among 193 centuries based upon age and property qualifications. The major **comitia**'s most prominent role was the election of public officials.

Comitium: The assembly area in front of the **Curia** where the general public was addressed from the **rostra**.

Confirmatio: Usually the fourth section of a speech in which the proofs are presented and the argument is developed.

Consul: The highest office in the **cursus honorum**, roughly equivalent to a mayor-president. Two people held the office each year.

Contio: A form of **comitia** in which all people were summoned without regard to group. Usually the **contio** convened near the **rostra** to hear debate on proposed legislation or an explanation of senatorial action.

Crescendo: The gradual building of words or phrases in order of importance or intensity. (223-226)

Curia: The Senate house.

Cursus Honorum: The customary sequence of elected offices (also called the **gradus honorum** at 265): **quaestor, aedile, praetor, consul**. Officially, one did not have to be an **aedile**, but most people elected to serve this office in order to garner votes for the remaining offices.

Dictator: Usually appointed in a state of emergency, the office lasted a maximum of six months and gave the holder absolute authority to settle a crisis. Originally known as the **magister populi**, "master of the infantry," he appointed the **magister equitum** as his chief assistant.

Ellipsis: The omission of words which must be understood from context. (45-47)

Equites (Equestrian): The wealthy middle class of businessmen.

Exordium: The introductory section of a speech.

Forum: The main marketplace in Rome and site of the law courts.

Hendiadys: "One through two," i.e., using two nouns to express one idea, an idea usually best translated by treating one noun as if it were an adjective modifying the other noun. (77)

Hostis: An enemy of the **res publica**, upon whom Rome could declare war and kill without trial.

Hyperbaton: The placement of an adjective far before the noun it modifies in order to emphasize the intensity of the adjective. (101-103)

Hyperbole: A gross exaggeration to make a point, but not to be taken literally. (83)

Irony: Saying one thing and meaning the opposite. (221-223)

Juxtaposition: "A placing side by side" of two elements for contrast and emphasis. (204-205)

Litotes: Using two negatives to make a vague positive. (142)

Magister Equitum: "The Master of the Cavalry" who was appointed by a **dictator** to represent his authority either on the field of battle or at Rome.

Metaphor: An implied comparison without the use of "like" or "as." (118)

Metonymy: Naming one thing by something closely associated with it. (82)

Narratio: Usually the second section of a speech in which the facts of the situation are laid out.

Nobiles: The class of families who had a consul among their ancestors.

Nobilitas: The political clout a family accrued first from having a consul among their ancestors and second from the "name recognition" and political ties (**amicitia**) that usually ensured political advancement.

Novae Tabellae: "New tables," meaning a cancellation of all debts.

Novus Homo: The first man in his family to rise in the **cursus honorum** to the level of **praetor** or **consul**, or the first family member to become a senator.

Optimates: "The best men," meaning the aristocratic group of **patricians** who wished for the true power in the Roman government to reside with the Senate, not the popular assemblies.

Oxymoron: The use of two logically contradictory adjectives or terms to describe the same noun. (170)

Palatine: The hill to the south of the **Forum** in Rome where the wealthiest people lived.

Pater Patriae: "Father of the Fatherland," an honorific title first given to Cicero after stopping Catiline, but later adopted by Julius Caesar, Augustus and some emperors.

Patres (Patrician): The moneyed upper class who were officially not allowed to engage in business.

Period (Periodic Sentence): A long sentence in which the main idea is delayed until the end after a series of related thoughts. The balancing of nouns, adjectives, verbs, or whole clauses lends greater emphasis and complexity to the main thought. (223-226)

Peroratio: The conclusion of a speech, often in the form of a prayer or request.

Persona: The personality of the author or speaker in a literary or oratorical context. This personality must be inferred from the **tone** and **style**.

Personification: Giving human characteristics to non-human beings or objects. (170-179)

Plebs (Plebeian): The lower class of Roman citizens not among the **equestrian** or **patrician** order.

Pomerium: The sacred area marking the official boundary of Rome, inside of which no armed forces were allowed while the city was secure.

Pontifex Maximus: The chief priest in Rome who was an elected official responsible for overseeing the major priestly colleges and the Vestal Virgins.

Popularis: Literally, "of the people." This adjective described any attempt to curry favor with or enact policy through the people rather than the Senate.

Praeteritio: Claiming that a point will not be mentioned but mentioning it anyway. This technique allows the speaker to introduce marginally relevant information in an attempt to prove a point by innuendo rather than by evidence. (20-22)

Praetor: The third office in the **cursus honorum**; the responsibilities pertained to the courts; similar to a modern judgeship.

Propositio: Usually the third section of a speech in which the points of agreement and contention are enumerated.

Propraetor: A term describing the governor of a province who was a **praetor** in Rome the previous year.

Quaestor: The first office in the **cursus honorum**; responsibilites included overseeing money and accounts in either Rome or a province.

Refutatio: Usually the fifth section of a speech in which arguments against the opponent's stance are presented.

Rhetoric/Rhetorical: A term derived from the Greek word for speaker, which has come to mean the art or skill of persuasion.

Rhetorical Question: A question to which no answer is expected; used to draw the audience into a particular line of thought, often without the expectation of careful analysis of the logical argument. (4-11)

Rostra: The speakers' platform in the **Forum**, to which were attached the prows of captured ships.

Senatus Consultum Ultimum: "The final decree of the Senate" which declared a state of emergency. The **consuls** were granted extraordinary powers to eliminate threats to the Republic — including the power to override other laws or to violate the rights of citizens. Thus, the decree is roughly equivalent to a declaration of martial law. The **consuls**, however, could be brought to censure after leaving office if they acted too strongly against politically powerful people.

Simile: A comparison using "like" or "as." (36-37)

Style: The author's characteristic use of **diction** and **figures of speech** for a specific effect.

Suo Anno: Election to the consulship at the youngest eligible age, i.e., 43 years of age.

Syncopation: The dropping of an unaccented syllable in the middle of a word. (110)

Synecdoche: Naming something by a part instead of the whole. (112)

Toga Virilis: The plain white toga worn by most citizens.

Tribune of the Plebs: Ten in number, these magistrates had the power of **veto** over any decrees of the Senate or legislation passed by the **comitia**. The office was originally designed to protect **plebeian** interests.

Tricolon: A grouping of three words or phrases at the summation of a point. (101)

Tullianum: In the prison next to the **Curia** this was the lowest chamber where executions took place.

Veto: The power of the **tribune of the plebs** to bar any senatorial legislation from becoming law.

IN L. CATILINAM
ORATIO PRIMA

Vocabulary, Notes, and Text

Vocabulary

abutor abuti abusus sum *w/ abl.* to abuse

arbitror *1* to think, suppose

audacia -ae *f.* boldness, recklessness

caedes -is *f.* slaughter, murder

concursus -us *m.* gathering

coniuratio -onis *f.* conspiracy

consilium -i *n.* debate; **consilium capere** to adopt a plan

constrictus/a/um (< **constringo**) bound, choked off

convoco *1* to call together

designo *1* to point out

effrenatus/a/um unbridled, unrestrained

eludo eludere elusi elusum to mock

etiam *adv.* still

fio fieri factus sum *irr. pass.* to be made, become

furor furoris *m.* madness

iacto *1* to throw about; **se iactare** to brag, boast

immo *adv.* no, rather

munitissimus/a/um most fortified

noto *1* to mark (down)

os oris *n.* mouth, face

particeps -cipis *m. w/ gen.* participant in

pateo patere patui to lie out in the open, be obvious

proximus/a/um last

quam diu *adv.* how long

quisque quidque each, every

quo *adv.* (to) where?

scientia -ae *f.* knowledge

sentio -ire sensi sensum to notice, perceive

sese (< **sui sibi**) *intensive form; tr. the same as* **se**.

superior -ius (< **superus**) *comp. adj.* before last

usque *adv.* all the way

vigilia -ae *f.* night watch

vito *1* to avoid

vultus -us *m.* face, expression

Notes

2 **In L. Catilinam**: **In** with a person in the accusative means "against" or "versus" in the legal sense. If this were a court, Cicero would be the prosecutor and Catiline the defendant.
L.: = Lucium, but translate using the nominative, Lucius. In Latin, every name declines, just as every other noun does, but in an English translation the nominative form is always used. All first name abbreviations are listed both in the complete vocabulary and in the table on page 50.

3 **Habita**: Translate with **oratio**. The standard Latin idiom for "to give a speech" is **orationem habere**.
In Senatu: "In a meeting of the Senate," or "Before the Senate." This does not indicate the actual place of the meeting. The Senate usually met in the **Curia**, but for reasons Cicero later explains, this meeting was held in the temple of Jupiter Stator.

4 **Quo usque tandem**: "How long, tell me, ..." (literally, "how far at length").
abutere: Second person, future, indicative. For explanation of form, see notes at 49 and 58. Remember that **utor** and its compounds govern a word in the ablative case (here, **patientia**). Note that Cicero begins with six **rhetorical questions**, three short and three long.

6-8 **nihilne**: "In no way at all ... ?" This **nihil** and the following ones are adverbial. The repetition of a word at the beginning of successive phrases is called **anaphora**.

6 **te**: Direct object of **moverunt** in 8.

[I] [1] Quo usque tandem abutere, Catilina, patientia nostra? quam diu etiam

furor iste tuus nos eludet? quem ad finem sese effrenata iactabit audacia?

Nihilne te nocturnum praesidium Palati, nihil urbis vigiliae, nihil timor populi,

nihil concursus bonorum omnium, nihil hic munitissimus habendi senatus locus,

nihil horum ora vultusque moverunt? Patere tua consilia non sentis, constrictam

iam horum omnium scientia teneri coniurationem tuam non vides? Quid proxima,

quid superiore nocte egeris, ubi fueris, quos convocaveris, quid consili ceperis,

quem nostrum ignorare arbitraris?

[2] O tempora, O mores! Senatus haec intellegit, consul videt; hic tamen vivit.

Vivit? immo vero etiam in senatum venit, fit publici consili particeps, notat et

designat oculis ad caedem unum quemque nostrum. Nos autem, fortes viri,

satis facere rei publicae videmur, si istius furorem ac tela vitamus.

---

7   **habendi senatus**: Genitive case with **locus**. **Habendi** is a gerundive modifying **senatus**.

8   **Patere**: An infinitive in indirect statement after **sentis**.

8-9   **constrictam ... teneri**: Cicero uses a participle and a passive infinitive where English would use two verbs joined by a conjunction. Translate as "choked off and held (back)."

9-11   Here are five indirect questions (**quid proxima ... quid consili**) followed by the direct question (**quem nostrum ignorare arbitraris**?). The translation will still make sense if it preserves the Latin order of the clauses.

9-10   **proxima ... superiore**: November 7 and 6, respectively.

10-11   **quid consili ... quem nostrum**: **Consili** and **nostrum** are partitive genitives.

12   **O tempora, O mores!**: Accusatives of exclamation. In English, some say "What's the world coming to?"

13   **etiam**: This is the second use of **etiam** we have met (see 4). **Etiam**, according to context, means "still," "even," or "also."

14   **unum quemque**: "Each and every one."
      fortes viri: Cicero must have uttered these words with strong **irony**.

15   **videmur**: Remember that the passive of **video** often means "seem."

---

acerbus/a/um bitter, severe

an *conj. (between two questions)* Or is it that ...?

aperte *adv.* openly

auctoritas -atis *f.* lead, support

coërceo -ere -ui -itum to repress, restrain

confero conferre contuli collatum to bring together

consilium -i *n.* plan of action

consultum -i *n.* decree

desum deesse defui *irr. v. w/ dat.* to fail

iam *adv. w/ past tense* already

iam diu *adv.* for a long time now

in *w/ acc. of person* against

incendium -i *n.* fire; *pl.* arson

iussu (< iussus) *abl. sg.* by order, at the command

labefacto *1* to weaken

machinor *1* to devise, plan

mediocriter *adv.* moderately, not very much

nimis *adv.* too, too much

novae res *f. pl.* revolution

occido occidere occidi occisum to kill, murder

oportet oportere oportuit *impers. in pres. tense* it is right, ought; *in past tenses* "ought to have <u>inf.</u> -ed"

orbis orbis *m.* globe; orbis terrae the world

ordo ordinis *m.* class, body

perfero -ferre -tuli -latum to put up with

perniciosus/a/um dangerous, destructive

pestis -is *f.* plague; destruction

pontifex pontificis *m.* priest

praetereo -ire -ivi (-ii) -itum to pass over

pridem *adv.* for a long time

privatus -i *m.* civilian, private citizen

quondam *adv.* at one time, formerly

status -us *m.* situation, condition

studeo studere studui *w/ dat.* to be eager for

supplicium -i *n.* punishment

vasto *1* to destroy

vehemens -ntis strong, forceful

vero *adv.* indeed

16 **duci ... oportebat**: A tricky construction. The basic Latin construction is **oportet** with the accusative and infinitive : "it is right for <u>acc.</u> to <u>inf.</u>." This is not a problem, until **oportet** is in a past tense. **Oportebat** as a main verb, translated as "ought," causes the Latin present infinitive to be translated as an English perfect infinitive ("to have (been) <u>verb</u> -ed"; the "been" translates a passive infinitive). Further, translate the accusative as the subject of the impersonal **oportebat**. Thus **te duci oportebat** = "You ought to have been led ...."

17 **conferri pestem**: Repeat the **oportebat** (16) and translate **pestem** as its subject.
omnis: Here this is an accusative plural modifying **nos**. For all third declension adjectives, **-is** is the alternative accusative plural ending. In all cases where the alternative **-is** is used, the "i" is long.
machinaris: Translate as a present perfect progressive, "have been planning."

18 **P. ... Ti.**: **P. = Publius**; **Ti. = Tiberium**, but remember to use the nominative in translation, i.e., Publius and Tiberius (cf. 2 and note). Publius Scipio Nasca, **consul** in 138 B.C., led the attack on Tiberius Gracchus in 133 B.C., the year in which Gracchus was **tribune of the plebs**. Gracchus had the people vote one of his colleagues out of office and was planning to run for a second consecutive term. The Senate thought Gracchus was aiming for too much power; thus Nasca led the attack, but he most likely did not kill Gracchus.
mediocriter: Notice the contrast between Tiberius Gracchus and Catiline. Tiberius was only causing a little trouble and was assassinated; Catiline, however, is plotting much more.

19 **interfecit: Catilinam**: Ignore the colon in translation and replace it with "and."

Ad mortem te, Catilina, duci iussu consulis iam pridem oportebat, in te   16
conferri pestem quam tu in nos omnis iam diu machinaris. [3] An vero vir   17
amplissimus, P. Scipio, pontifex maximus, Ti. Gracchum mediocriter   18
labefactantem statum rei publicae privatus interfecit: Catilinam orbem terrae   19
caede atque incendiis vastare cupientem nos consules perferemus? Nam illa   20
nimis antiqua praetereo, quod C. Servilius Ahala Sp. Maelium novis rebus   21
studentem manu sua occidit.   22

Fuit, fuit ista quondam in hac re publica virtus ut viri fortes acrioribus   23
suppliciis civem perniciosum quam acerbissimum hostem coërcerent. Habemus   24
senatus consultum in te, Catilina, vehemens et grave; non deest rei publicae   25
consilium neque auctoritas huius ordinis: nos, nos, dico aperte, consules   26
desumus.   27

19-20 **Catilinam ... cupientem**: **Cupientem** modifies **Catilinam**. Latin often places the participle at the end of a participial phrase in much the same way a finite verb indicates the end of a subordinate clause. To the Roman ear, everything between the noun and participle belongs to the participial phrase. Here, then, **vastare** is a complementary infinitive with **cupientem**, and **orbem** is the object of **vastare**.

21 **praetereo**: An example of **praeteritio**. Cicero claims he will not mention a marginally relevant historical episode, but then he mentions it anyway.
quod: "... the fact that."

21-22 **C. Servilius Ahala Sp. Maelium ... occidit**: **C.** = **Gaius**; **Sp.** = **Spurium** (cf. 2 and 17). The clause is an historical **allusion**. Ahala, Cincinnatus's **magister equitum**, killed the **plebeian** Maelius in 440 B.C. when Maelius was accused of selling grain inexpensively during a famine in order to gain political support.

23 **Fuit, fuit**: The repetition heightens the emotional pitch of the speech.
ista: Here **ista** serves as a signal word for a result clause, much as **tantus** or **ita** usually does.

24 **quam**: "Than" after the comparative **acrioribus** (23).

25 **senatus consultum**: A reference to the **senatus consultum ultimum** passed by the Senate on October 21 (see *Catiline and Conspiracy*, page x, and the *Glossary of Terms and Figures of Speech*, page xvi).
rei publicae: Dative governed by **desum**.

26 **nos, nos**: Note the repetition of **fuit** (23) and **nos** as Cicero contrasts the present failure of the Senate and consuls to act against Catiline with the historical precedents.

acies -ei *f.* sharpness, edge

avus avi *m.* grandfather

confestim *adv.* immediately

confirmo *1* to strengthen

consularis -e of consular rank

consultum -i *n.* decree

convenio -ire -veni -ventum *impers. v.* it is fitting, proper

decerno -ere decrevi decretum to vote, decree

detrimentum -i *n.* loss, harm; **detrimentum capere** = to receive harm

hebesco -ere *def. v.* to grow dull

includo -ere -clusi -clusum to enclose

intercedo -cedere -cessi -cessum to pass

liberi -orum *m. pl.* children

maiores maiorum (< **magnus/a/um**) *m. pl. subst.* ancestors

modus -i *m.* sort, type

num *interr. adv.* "_subject_ didn't ..., did _subject_?"

permitto -ere -misi -missum to entrust _acc._ to _dat._

plebs plebis *f.* common people

praetor -is *m.* praetor

recondo -ere -condidi -conditum to hide, conceal

remoror *1* to wait on

seditio seditionis *f.* insurrection, rebellion

suspicio -onis *f.* suspicion

tabula -ae *f.* tablet; *pl.* (public) records

tribunus -i *m.* tribune

uti *conj. same as* **ut**

vagina -ae *f.* sheath, scabbard

verum *conj.* but

vicesimus/a/um twentieth

---

28   **uti ... videret**: A jussive noun clause that explains what the Senate decreed.
ne quid: = **ne aliquid**. The Romans dropped the **ali-** prefix when forms of **aliquis** followed **ne**, **nisi**, **num**, or **si**. The word retained its meaning "someone, something." A convenient mnemonic device for the list of words is "after **si**, **nisi**, **num**, and **ne**, **ali-** takes a holiday."

28-29   **consul ... caperet**: This is the phrasing of the **senatus consultum ultimum** (see 25 and note). Here Cicero cites the first time the **senatus consultum ultimum** was passed, that is, during Opimius's consulship in 121 B.C. This decree granted the **consul** extraordinary power against private citizens. Later, Opimius was brought up on charges of murdering Roman citizens without proper trial in spite of the fact that he was acting under a **senatus consultum ultimum**. Although Opimius was acquitted, Cicero has just reason to fear that his enemies may later attack him in the courts if he acts too hastily against Catiline.

29   **detrimenti**: Partitive genitive with **quid** (28).

30   **clarissimo ... maioribus**: Ablatives of description with **C. Gracchus**.

31   **M. Fulvius consularis**: Marcus Fulvius Flaccus had been **consul** in 125 B.C. Thus, he is rightly called **consularis**, but it is quite remarkable that he held the office of **tribune of the plebs** in 122 B.C. after his consulship. His sons were also killed, one of them most unjustly, and they stand as an example of Opimius's cruelty.
Simili ... consulto: Ablative of means.

[II] [4] Decrevit quondam senatus uti L. Opimius consul videret ne quid res publica   28

detrimenti caperet: nox nulla intercessit; interfectus est propter quasdam   29

seditionum suspiciones C. Gracchus, clarissimo patre, avo, maioribus, occisus   30

est cum liberis M. Fulvius consularis. Simili senatus consulto C. Mario et L.   31

Valerio consulibus est permissa res publica: num unum diem postea L.   32

Saturninum tribunum plebis et C. Servilium praetorem mors ac rei publicae   33

poena remorata est?   34

At vero nos vicesimum iam diem patimur hebescere aciem horum auctoritatis.   35

Habemus enim eius modi senatus consultum, verum inclusum in tabulis,   36

tamquam in vagina reconditum, quo ex senatus consulto confestim te interfectum   37

esse, Catilina, convenit. Vivis, et vivis non ad deponendam, sed ad confirmandam   38

audaciam.   39

31-32 **C. Mario ... consulibus**: Datives governed by the verb **est permissa**. This establishes the date as 100 B.C.

32 **num**: This is virtually an untranslatable word, but in Latin **num** introduces a question that expects the answer "no."
unum diem: "For one day." Accusative of duration of time.

33-34 **rei publicae poena**: "Capital punishment." Here the **poena** is death.

35 **iam**: "Already."

36 **eius modi**: "Of this type." Cicero means the **senatus consultum ultimum** already mentioned in 25 and 28-29.

37 **tamquam**: The **simile** emphasizes the neglected power of the **consultum**.
quo ex senatus consulto: In English the word order becomes **ex quo consulto senatus**. Translate **ex** as "according to."

38-39 **ad deponendam ... audaciam**: **ad** with gerund/gerundive expresses purpose. Translate as "for _verb_ -ing _noun_." Note the **antithesis** of **deponendam** and **confirmandam**.

adduco -ere -duxi -ductum to prompt, induce

adeo *adv.* all the way, right up to

clemens -ntis merciful

colloco *1* to station, place

comprehendo -ere -prehendi -prehensum to sieze, arrest

condemno *1 w/ gen.* to find <u>acc.</u> guilty of <u>gen.</u>

conscripti *in the phrase* **patres conscripti** *voc. pl.* senators

cotidie *adv.* every day

cresco -ere crevi cretum to grow, increase

dissolutus/a/um irresponsible

Etruria -ae *f.* Etruria (the district northwest of Rome)

fauces faucium *f. pl.* pass (of a mountain)

iam pridem *adv.* long ago

inertia -ae *f.* laziness, neglect

intestinus/a/um internal

moenia -ium *n. pl.* walls of a city, defenses

molior moliri molitus sum to try, attempt

nequitia -ae *f.* worthlessness

pernicies -ei *f.* destruction, threat

potius ... quam *conj.* rather than

serius (< **serus**) *comp. adv.* too late

singuli/ae/a *distributive pl.* each

vereor -eri veritus sum to fear, be afraid

verum *conj.* but

---

42   **collocata**: Agrees with **castra**. The camp is Manlius's at Faesulae in northern Etruria.

43   **in dies singulos**: "With each and every day."

45   **molientem**: Agrees with **imperatorem ducemque** in 43-44.
      iam: "at once."

46   **iussero**: This is the finite verb for both "**si**" clauses. Repeat when translating.

46-47   **credo ... dicat**: Cicero has left out many words here, a figure called **ellipsis**. The basic construction is a fear clause. For example: **vereor ne miles Romanus veniat**. ("I fear that the Roman soldier is coming.") He has added two variations to this basic construction. First, he has compared two different fears with the conjunction **potius ... quam**. Second, he has added a **non** after the **ne**, but it makes most sense to translate the **non** just before the **ne**. Here is a breakdown of the clauses in a word order more natural to English. Latin words supplied to fill out the meaning are in parentheses.

        [Main]   credo, erit verendum mihi

           [Fear 1]   non ne hoc omnes boni serius a me (factum esse dicant)

        [Conjunction] potius quam

           [Fear 2]   (ne) quisquam (hoc) crudelius (a me) factum esse dicat.

"I suppose I will have to fear, not that all the upstanding citizens will say that this was done too late by me, but rather that anyone at all will say that this was done too cruelly."

Cupio, patres conscripti, me esse clementem, cupio in tantis rei publicae   40
periculis non dissolutum videri, sed iam me ipse inertiae nequitiaeque condemno.   41
[5] Castra sunt in Italia contra populum Romanum in Etruriae faucibus collocata,   42
crescit in dies singulos hostium numerus; eorum autem castrorum imperatorem   43
ducemque hostium intra moenia atque adeo in senatu videtis intestinam aliquam   44
cotidie perniciem rei publicae molientem. Si te iam, Catilina, comprehendi, si   45
interfici iussero, credo, erit verendum mihi ne non hoc potius omnes boni serius   46
a me quam quisquam crudelius factum esse dicat. Verum ego hoc quod iam   47
pridem factum esse oportuit certa de causa nondum adducor ut faciam.   48

---

47   **quisquam**: As a final point, **quisquam** is usually found in negative clauses with the sense "any-one at all." Thus Cicero implies that, while he does not fear that the upstanding citizens will criticize him, there is hardly anyone at all who could be found to say that he acted too cruelly. This is an **ironic** statement given the fact that Cicero has already rebuked himself for not taking action soon enough, a delay that caused an increased threat to the state (cf. the **castra** in 42). Further, Cicero does fear that people will say he acted too harshly (cf. 28-29 and note).

48   **oportuit**: See note at 16.

47-48   **Verum ... faciam**: Again, this sentence makes better sense after dividing it into clauses:

      [Main]   verum ego hoc
           [Relative]   quod iam pridem factum esse oportuit
      [Main]   certa de causa nondum adducor
           [Result]   ut faciam.

Notice how the main clause is broken into segments. Interrupting a clause with other clauses is common in both Latin and English; but, whenever an unfinished clause (here the main clause) is interrupted by another clause or group of clauses, the first clause cannot continue until the interrupting clause is complete. Accordingly, here Cicero finishes the relative clause before returning to the main clause. When translating, the Latin word order may be closely followed.

adhuc *adv.* up to this point

amplius (< amplus) *comp. adj./adv.* more

audeo -ere ausus sum *semi-dep.* to dare

auris -is *f.* ear

caedes -is *f.* slaughter, murder

coetus -us *m.* meeting

commoveo -ere -movi -motum to move, rouse

custodio -ire -ivi -itum to guard, watch over

erumpo -ere -rupi -ruptum to break out

etenim *conj.* and indeed, and really

exspecto *1* to wait for, await, expect

fateor -eri fassus sum to claim

firmus/a/um secure, reliable

illustro *1* to reveal, disclose

improbus/a/um wicked, shameless

incendium -i *n.* fire; *pl.* arson

iure (< ius) *abl. sg.* rightly, justly

licet licere licuit *impers. v.* it is permitted

muto *1* to change

nefarius/a/um unspeakable, wicked

obliviscor -i oblitus sum *w/ gen.* to forget

obscuro *1* to cover up

obsessus/a/um (< obsideo) besieged, surrounded

oculus -i *m.* eye

paries parietis *m.* wall (of a house)

perditus/a/um (< perdo) lost, corrupt

quam diu *conj.* as long as

recognosco -ere -cognovi -cognitum to recall, recount, review

sicut *conj.* just as

speculor *1* to watch

tenebrae -arum *f. pl.* darkness

undique *adv.* from everywhere, on all sides

ut *conj. w/ indicative* as, when

---

49   **interficiere**: Second person, future, passive (cf. 4). The alternative second person passive ending for **-ris** is **-re** and is most frequently used with future verbs. Note the possiblity for confusion between this and the present active infinitive (**interficere**), although the forms are different. Also, there is an ambiguity in the written forms of the present and future tenses in the third conjugation; in spoken Latin, however, the future is easily discerned by the long "e" before the **-re**.
iam nemo: "No longer anyone."
tui: Genitive with **similis** (50).

50   **poterit**: **Cum** clauses have indicative verbs when the **cum** clause refers to one specific time.
qui: = **ut is**. Relative clause of result.
quisquam: See note on 47. Cicero is again asserting the unlikelihood of Catiline having any supporters.

53   **sentientem**: Present active participle agreeing with **te** (52).

55   **amplius**: Translate outside of its clause immediately after the preceding **quid**.
exspectes: Subjunctive in a relative clause of characteristic.

Tum denique interficiere, cum iam nemo tam improbus, tam perditus, tam tui 49

similis inveniri poterit qui id non iure factum esse fateatur. [6] Quam diu quisquam 50

erit qui te defendere audeat, vives, et vives ita ut nunc vivis, multis meis et firmis 51

praesidiis obsessus, ne commovere te contra rem publicam possis. Multorum te 52

etiam oculi et aures non sentientem, sicut adhuc fecerunt, speculabuntur atque 53

custodient. 54

[III] Etenim quid est, Catilina, quod iam amplius exspectes, si neque nox tenebris 55

obscurare coetus nefarios nec privata domus parietibus continere voces 56

coniurationis tuae potest, si illustrantur, si erumpunt omnia? Muta iam istam 57

mentem, mihi crede, obliviscere caedis atque incendiorum. Teneris undique; 58

luce sunt clariora nobis tua consilia omnia, quae iam mecum licet recognoscas. 59

55-56   **nox ... domus**: Both are subjects of **potest**.

56   **parietibus**: "By." Ablative of instrument.

57   **omnia**: Subject of both **illustrantur** and **erumpunt**.

58   **obliviscere**: Deponent imperative. Another confusing **-re** form. For the sake of summary, **-re** may terminate the following forms:

       For regular active verbs:

           1. Pres., act., infinitive
           2. 2nd pers., sg., pres., pass., indicative/subjunctive = **-ris**
           3. 2nd pers., sg., fut., pass., indicative = **-ris**

       For deponents:
           4. 2nd pers., sg., pres., imperative
           5. 2nd pers., sg., pres., subjunctive/indicative = **-ris**
           6. 2nd pers., sg., fut., indicative = **-ris**

59   **licet recognoscas**: = **licet tibi recognoscere**.

administer -tri *m.* assistant

admiror *1* to wonder at, admire

atrox atrocis cruel

ceteri/ae/a the rest, everybody (everything) else

circumcludo -ere -clusi -clusum to shut in, surround

colonia -ae *f.* colony

confero conferre contuli collatum to assign

confido -ere -fisus sum *semi-dep.* to trust, be confident

contentus/a/um (< contineo) content, satisfied

diligentia -ae *f.* attention, energy

discessus -us *m.* departure, withdrawal

fallo -ere fefelli falsum to deceive

idem *adv.* likewise

impetus -us *m.* attack

infitior *1* to deny, contradict

iussu (< iussus) *abl. sg.* by order, at the command

Kalendae -arum *f. pl.* the Kalends, the first of the month

magis *adv.* more, rather

memini meminisse *def. v. w/ gen.* to remember

molior -iri molitus sum to try, attempt

multo *adv.* by far, far

November/bris/bre of November

optimates optimatium *m. pl.* the optimates, the aristocratic party

Praeneste -is *n.* Praeneste (a town twenty miles east of Rome)

princeps principis *m. subst.* chief; principes civitatis leading citizens

profugio -ere -fugi to flee, escape

reprimo -ere -pressi -pressum to restrain, check

satelles satellitis *m./f. attendant,* accomplice

tam ... quam *conj.* so much ... as

verum *conj.* but

---

60   me ... dicere: "My saying."
ante diem XII Kalendas Novembris: = "On October 21."
Novembris: Modifying Kalendas. The -is is the third declension alternative ending for the accusative plural (cf. 17 and note).
fore: = futurum esse (future infinitive of sum). C. Manlius (61) is the subject of fore. The direct statement of fore would be erit.

61   qui dies: The qui agrees with the dies that follows it and refers to the die that comes before. Cicero keeps repeating dies to emphasize the accuracy of his knowledge of the "secret" conspiracy.
Kal.: = Kalendas
ante diem VI Kal. Novembris: October 27.

62   audaciae satellitem atque administrum tuae: Chiasmus.

64   caedem te ... contulisse: In order to make sense, the subject of contulisse must be te.

64-65 ante diem V Kalendas Novembris: October 28. Translate: "You had decided upon October 28 for the slaughter ...."

65   Roma: Ablative of separation with profugerunt (66).

65-66 sui conservandi ... causa: "for the sake of <u>verb</u>-ing the <u>noun/pronoun</u>." An expression of purpose with the gerund/gerundive.

[7] Meministine me ante diem XII Kalendas Novembris dicere in senatu fore 60

in armis certo die, qui dies futurus esset ante diem VI Kal. Novembris, C. Manlium, 61

audaciae satellitem atque administrum tuae? Num me fefellit, Catilina, non modo 62

res tanta, tam atrox tamque incredibilis, verum, id quod multo magis est admirandum, 63

dies? Dixi ego idem in senatu caedem te optimatium contulisse in ante diem 64

V Kalendas Novembris, tum cum multi principes civitatis Roma non tam sui 65

conservandi quam tuorum consiliorum reprimendorum causa profugerunt. 66

Num infitiari potes te illo ipso die meis praesidiis, mea diligentia circumclusum 67

commovere te contra rem publicam non potuisse, cum tu discessu ceterorum 68

nostra tamen qui remansissemus caede contentum te esse dicebas? [8] Quid? cum 69

te Praeneste Kalendis ipsis Novembribus occupaturum nocturno impetu esse 70

confideres, sensistin illam coloniam meo iussu meis praesidiis, custodiis, vigiliis 71

esse munitam? Nihil agis, nihil moliris, nihil cogitas quod non ego non modo 72

audiam sed etiam videam planeque sentiam. 73

---

67   **praesidiis ... diligentia**: Ablatives of means with **circumclusum**.

68   **commovere te**: **Commovere** is transitive, which means it must have a direct object in Latin. Omit the second **te** in translation.

69   **nostra tamen qui**: The antecedent of **qui** is a **nos** implied by **nostra**. **Nostra** agrees with **caede**. (Translation hint: "by the slaughter of us who ....")
      Quid: This calls attention to the question that follows. "And furthermore" or "Tell me."

70   **Praeneste**: Accusative direct object of **occupaturum ... esse**.
      Kalendis ipsis Novembribus: November 1.

71   **sensistin**: = sensistine.
      praesidiis ... vigiliis: Notice how Cicero leaves out conjunctions as his emotional pitch increases. This keeps the speech moving along and has a "rapid-fire" effect. Omission of conjunctions is called **asyndeton**.

72   **nihil ... nihil**: Anaphora (cf. 6-8 and note) and **tricolon**.

72-73 **non ... non modo ... sed etiam**: The first **non** negates the following three verbs (**audiam**, **videam** and **sentiam**) and can be repeated in translation with each. By placing the **non** immediately after the **quod**, Cicero is effectively making the **quod** another **nihil**. The second **non** serves in the common correlative construction **non modo ... sed etiam**. Note the numerous three-word phrases in this paragraph that build to a **climax** with **sentiam**.

acrius *comp. adv.* more harshly

adeo *adv.* even, in fact

amentia -ae *f.* madness, folly

apud *prep. w/ acc. of person* at the house of

complures compluria (complura) several, many

convinco -ere -vici -victum to prove wrong

deligo -ere -legi -lectum to choose

discribo -ere -scripsi -scriptum to describe

distribuo -ere -tribui -tributum to divide, assign

eodem *adv.* in the same place

exeo -ire -ii -itum to go out, leave

exitium -i *n.* ruin, destruction

falcarii -orum *m. pl.* Scythemakers' Street (a neighborhood in Rome)

ferrum -i *n.* iron; *fig.* sword

hic *adv.* here

iam *adv. w/ future tense* soon

incendium -i *n.* fire; *pl.* arson

interitus -us *m.* ruin, death, destruction

lectus -i *m.* bed, couch

mora -ae *f.* delay

multo *adv.* far, much

orbis orbis *m.* circle, globe; **orbis terrae**, the world

paulum -i *n.* a little bit

placet placere placuit *impers. v.* it is pleasing

polliceor -eri pollicitus sum to promise

prior prius *comp. adj.* before last

quidam quaedam quoddam (quiddam) *indef. pron./adj.* certain, some

reperio -ire -pperi -pertum to find

rogo *1* to ask; **sententiam rogare** to ask the opinion of <u>acc.</u>

salus salutis *f.* safety

sententia -ae *f.* thought, opinion

statuo -ere statui statutum to decide

superior -ius (< superus) *comp. adj.* before last

taceo -ere tacui tacitum to be quiet, silent

tandem *adv.* at length, finally

trucido *1* to slaughter, butcher

ubinam gentium where in the world

una *adv.* together

vigilo *1* to be attentive

vulnero *1* to harm; offend

---

74   **noctem illam superiorem**: "That night before last." November 6.

75   **rei publicae**: Genitive, both with **salutem** and with **perniciem**.

76   **agam**: = **loquar**.
       M. Laecae: = **Marci Laecae**. All we know for certain about Marcus Porcius Laeca is that he was a senator.

77   **convenisse**: Infinitive in indirect discourse after **dico** in 75.
       compluris: Accusative plural modifying **socios** (cf. 17, 60, etc.).
       amentiae scelerisque: "Wicked folly." This **hendiadys** gives **sceleris** the force of an adjective modifying **amentiae**.

78   **Quid**: = **Cur**.

82   **consilio**: "Meeting." By **metonymy**, the debate comes to mean the meeting of the Senate.
       nostro omnium interitu: = **interitu omnium nostrum**. Note the **hyperbole** in this and the following line.

[IV] Recognosce tandem mecum noctem illam superiorem; iam intelleges multo   74
me vigilare acrius ad salutem quam te ad perniciem rei publicae. Dico te priore   75
nocte venisse inter falcarios — non agam obscure — in M. Laecae domum;   76
convenisse eodem compluris eiusdem amentiae scelerisque socios. Num negare   77
audes? quid taces? Convincam, si negas. Video enim esse hic in senatu quosdam   78
qui tecum una fuerunt.   79

[9] O di immortales! ubinam gentium sumus? quam rem publicam habemus?   80
in qua urbe vivimus? Hic, hic sunt in nostro numero, patres conscripti, in hoc   81
orbis terrae sanctissimo gravissimoque consilio, qui de nostro omnium interitu,   82
qui de huius urbis atque adeo de orbis terrarum exitio cogitent.   Hos ego video   83
consul et de re publica sententiam rogo, et quos ferro trucidari oportebat, eos   84
nondum voce vulnero!   85

Fuisti igitur apud Laecam illa nocte, Catilina, distribuisti partes Italiae,   86
statuisti quo quemque proficisci placeret, delegisti quos Romae relinqueres,   87
quos tecum educeres, discripsisti urbis partes ad incendia, confirmasti te   88
ipsum iam esse exiturum, dixisti paulum tibi esse etiam nunc morae, quod   89
ego viverem. Reperti sunt duo equites Romani qui te ista cura liberarent   90
et se illa ipsa nocte paulo ante lucem me in meo lecto interfecturos esse   91
pollicerentur.   92

84   **quos ... oportebat**: The antecedent of **quos** is the **eos** at the end of 84. For the sake of simplicity, translate the relative clause immediately after its antecedent. See the note on 16 for the translation of **oportebat**.

87   **quo ... placeret**: **Quo** introduces an indirect question ("where ...").
     quemque placeret: = **quisque cuperet**.

86-89   **distribuisti ... dixisti**: Notice that Cicero uses no conjunctions to connect the independent verbs (**asyndeton**).

88   **confirmasti**: = **confirmavisti** (**syncopation**).

89   **morae**: "Cause for delay."
     quod: "The fact that."

90-92   **qui ... pollicerentur**: "Who would free ... and (who) would promise ...." A relative clause of characteristic with purpose implied.

90   **ista cura**: Ablative of separation after **liberarent**.

aliquando *adv.* at some time, at last

coetus -us *m.* meeting, gathering

comperio -ire -peri -pertum to find out, discover

custos custodis *m./f.* guardian

desidero *1* to long for, miss

diutius (< **diu**) *comp. adv.* longer

egredior -i -gressus sum to go out, leave

excludo -ere -clusi -clusum to shut out

infestus/a/um hostile, dangerous

mane *adv.* early in the morning

Manlianus/a/um of Manlius

metus -us *m.* fear, anxiety

minus *comp. adv.* not

modo = dum modo *conj.* so long as, provided that

nimium *adv.* too, too much

pateo -ere patui to be open

pergo -ere perrexi perrectum to keep on, proceed, go forward

pestis pestis *f.* plague destruction

praedico -ere -dixi -dictum to foretell, predict

purgo *1* to cleanse, purify

saluto *1* to greet, pay respects to

sino -ere sivi situm to permit, allow

Stator -oris *m.* the Stayer (a name given to Jupiter)

taeter/tra/trum loathsome, foul

totiens *adv.* so many times

versor *1* to be among, be around

vixdum *adv.* hardly yet, barely

---

94   **salutatum**: "To greet." Accusative supine expressing purpose. Cicero here and with **lecto** in 91 is alluding to the **salutatio**, the morning greeting a group of clients (**clientela**) gave to their patron while he remained in bed.

94-95   **eos quos ... illi ipsi ... quos**: The same **equites** mentioned in 90.

95   **multis ... viris**: Dative indirect objects with **praedixeram** (96).

96   **id temporis**: = **eo tempore**.

97   **Quae cum ita sint**: "Since these things are so," or "under these circumstances." In this idiom, the coordinating relative **quae** is equivalent to **et haec** ("and these things"), and refers back to the facts stated in the previous section. Use of the relative pronoun as a coordinating conjunction is quite common.
    quo: "Where." **Quo** is used instead of **ubi** with a verb of motion. Literally, **quo** means "to where," or the rather archaic English word "whither," e.g., "Whither goest thou?"

98   **tua ... castra**: Cicero has turned Manlius's name into an adjective, a change that may sound pretentious in English: Marlon's book = the Marlonian book. **Illa** here refers to the camp at Faesulae, so "up there" is about as close to Cicero's effect as English can come: "Your and Manlius's camp up there."

[10] Haec ego omnia vixdum etiam coetu vestro dimisso comperi; domum meam 93
maioribus praesidiis munivi atque firmavi, exclusi eos quos tu ad me salutatum 94
mane miseras, cum illi ipsi venissent quos ego iam multis ac summis viris ad me 95
id temporis venturos esse praedixeram. 96

[V] Quae cum ita sint, Catilina, perge quo coepisti: egredere aliquando ex urbe; 97
patent portae; proficiscere. Nimium diu te imperatorem tua illa Manliana castra 98
desiderant. Educ tecum etiam omnis tuos, si minus, quam plurimos; purga 99
urbem. Magno me metu liberaveris, modo inter me atque te murus intersit. 100
Nobiscum versari iam diutius non potes; non feram, non patiar, non sinam. 101

[11] Magna dis immortalibus habenda est atque huic ipsi Iovi Statori, antiquissimo 102
custodi huius urbis, gratia, quod hanc tam taetram, tam horribilem tamque 103
infestam rei publicae pestem totiens iam effugimus. 104

---

99   **omnis**: Accusative plural (cf. 17, 60 etc.).
      quam plurimos: Remember that **quam** with the superlative = "as _adj._ as possible."

100   **Magno ... murus**: Note the alliteration of "m."

101   **iam diutius non**: "No longer" or "not anymore."
      non feram ... sinam: These words are not exactly synonymous, although each can have the meaning "to permit." Note the **tricolon**.

102-03 **Magna ... gratia**: **Magna** modifies **gratia**. Cicero has separated the adjective from the noun in order to emphasize his gratitude. Separation of an adjective from the noun it modifies is called **hyperbaton**.
      habenda est ... gratia: = **gratiae sunt agendae** (passive periphrastic).

104   **iam**: With perfect tense = "already."
      effugimus: Present perfect: "We have escaped."

aperte *adv.* openly

campus -i *m.* plain, marching field

comes comitis *m./f.* comrade, companion

comitia -orum *n. pl.* election

competitor -is *m.* rival, opponent

conatus -us *m.* attempt, undertaking

concito *1* to stir up, incite

coniungo -ere -iunxi -iunctum to join together

coniurati -orum *m. pl.* conspirators

consularis -e of consular rank, consular

designatus/a/um (< **designo**) elect

disciplina -ae *f.* training, instruction

dudum *adv.* some time, for a long time

exhaurio -ire -hausi -haustum to drain off, drink down

exitium -i *n.* destruction, ruin

insidior *1 w/ dat.* lie in wait for, plot against

lenis -e mild, gentle

maiores maiorum (< **magnus/a/um**) *m. pl. subst.* ancestors

manus -us *f.* gang

nefarius/a/um unspeakable, wicked

obsisto -ere obstiti obstitum *w/ dat.* to resist, thwart

periclitor *1* to put to the test, risk

peto -ere -ivi -itum to attack, aim at

proprius/a/um *w/ gen.* special to, appropriate for

proximus/a/um last, most recent

qua re and for this reason, therefore

quam diu *conj.* as long as

quoniam *conj.* since

quotienscumque *adv.* however often, whenever

reliquus/a/um left over, remaining

resideo -ere -sedi to stay behind, be left

saepius (< **saepe**) *comp. adv.* too often

sentina -ae *f.* bilge water, sewage, dregs

severitas -atis *f.* strict action, sternness

sin *conj.* but if, if on the contrary

tecta -orum *n. pl.* roofs; houses

tumultus -us *m.* riot

utilis -e useful, advantageous

vastitas -atis *f.* devastation, desolation, ruin

---

105 **in uno homine**: **In = propter**.
summa salus: "The very existence." **Salus** most often means a person's health and safety, and thus well-being. Here, Cicero uses the term more metaphorically to describe the Republic. The superlative **summa** emphasizes the very things that allow the Republic to be "healthy," i.e., due process in the assemblies and courts. Catiline's behavior is clearly a threat to these fundamental institutions.

106 **consuli designato**: 63 B.C. was the year of Cicero's consulship, so he was consul elect between the summer of 64 and January of 63.

107-08 **in campo**: The **Campus Martius**, site of the **comitia** and military drills. The plain was located between the **pomerium** and the Tiber river. Cicero, in fact, had already postponed the election once because of Catiline's threat.

109 **nullo ... concitato**: "When no riot had been incited." Ablative absolute. A **tumultus** here is an official recognition that a riot threatens the stability of the state.
denique: "In short."

110 **petisti**: Syncopated form of **petivisti**.
per me: "All by myself."

111 **Nunc iam**: "But right now."

Non est saepius in uno homine summa salus periclitanda rei publicae. Quam 105
diu mihi consuli designato, Catilina, insidiatus es, non publico me praesidio, sed 106
privata diligentia defendi. Cum proximis comitiis consularibus me consulem in 107
campo et competitores tuos interficere voluisti, compressi conatus tuos nefarios 108
amicorum praesidio et copiis nullo tumultu publice concitato; denique 109
quotienscumque me petisti, per me tibi obstiti, quamquam videbam perniciem 110
meam cum magna calamitate rei publicae esse coniunctam. [12] Nunc iam 111
aperte rem publicam universam petis, templa deorum immortalium, tecta 112
urbis, vitam omnium civium, Italiam totam ad exitium et vastitatem vocas. 113
Qua re, quoniam id quod est primum, et quod huius imperi disciplinaeque 114
maiorum proprium est, facere nondum audeo, faciam id quod est ad severitatem 115
lenius, ad communem salutem utilius. Nam si te interfici iussero, residebit in re 116
publica reliqua coniuratorum manus; sin tu, quod te iam dudum hortor, exieris, 117
exhaurietur ex urbe tuorum comitum magna et perniciosa sentina rei publicae. 118

---

112   **tecta**: Literally, "covered things" or "homes" by **synecdoche**.

113   **vitam**: Cicero uses the singular here because in Latin the plural **vitae** means "biographies."
       Translate as "lives."

114   **qua re**: "Therefore." Coordinating relative; see note at 97.

114-15 **quod est primum ... proprium est**: "That which would be first and appropriate to ...."
       huius imperi: "My command," that is, the power given to Cicero under the martial law
       imposed by the **senatus consultum ultimum**.

115-16 **ad ... ad**: Translate each **ad** as "with regard to."

117   **reliqua**: Modifies **manus** ("gang").
       quod: "Something which." The antecedent is the verbal idea expressed in **exieris**.
       iam dudum hortor: **Iam dudum, iam pridem**, etc., usually modify a present tense verb. In
       translation, the English verb becomes present perfect, e.g., "I have been encouraging for a
       long time now" (cf. 17).

118   **sentina**: A striking example of a **metaphor** to increase the vividness.

absum abesse afui afuturus *irr. v.* to be away

adulescentulus -i *m. diminutive* little young man

consulo -ere -sului -sultum to consult

corruptela -ae *f.* corruption, temptation

cumulo *1* to heap up

dedecus -oris *n.* disgrace

delecto *1* to please, delight

exsisto -ere exstiti exstitum to appear; exist

extra *prep. w/ acc.* outside of

facinus -oris *n.* deed; outrage

fax facis *f.* torch, firebrand

flagitium -i *n.* outrage, disgrace

haereo -ere haesi haesum to stick to, cling to

Idus Iduum *f. pl.* the Ides (15th of March, May, July, and October; 13th of other months)

ignominia -ae *f.* shame, dishonor

illecebra -ae *f.* enticement, charm

immanitas -atis *f.* enormity, ferocity

impendeo -ere *def. v. w/ dat.* to threaten

inuro -ere -ussi -ustum *w/ dat.* to burn in, brand upon

irretio -ire -retivi -retitum to catch in a net, ensnare

libido -inis *f.* desire, passion

metuo -ere metui to fear, be afraid of

nota -ae *f.* mark, brand

nuper *adv.* recently

nuptiae -arum *f. pl.* wedding, marriage

odi odisse *def. v. in perf. tenses only* to hate

perditus/a/um (< **perdo**) corrupt

praefero -ferre -tuli -latum to carry <u>acc.</u> before/in front of <u>dat.</u>

praetermitto -ere -misi -missum to pass over, leave out

ruina -ae *f.* ruin, destruction

sileo -ere -ui to be quiet, leave unmentioned

sponte (tua) *f. abl. sg. only* of your own accord, voluntarily

suadeo -ere suasi suasum *w/ dat. of pers.* to advise, urge

superior -ius (< **superus**) *comp. adj.* previous, last

turpitudo -inis *f.* disgrace, shame

vacuefacio -ere -feci -factum to make empty, clear

vindico *1* to avenge, punish

vitium -i *n.* crime, vice

---

119   **num**: "Surely, ... not ... ?"
       id ... quod: The "it" is Catiline's leaving and organizing a **coup d'état**.

120   **hostem**: By declaring Catiline an enemy of the state, as opposed to an **inimicus** (personal enemy), Cicero makes it easier for the Senate to justify harsh action against Catiline.

121   **num**: "Whether." This introduces an indirect question in which Cicero leaves out most of the question (**ellipsis**). The full question would have been **num in exsilium consul eum ire iubeat**.

122-24 **possit ... metuat ... oderit**: Either potential subjunctives or relative clauses of characteristic.

124   **domesticae**: Refers to the reputation and history of his family, including his relatives and their political alliances.
       inusta: Cicero alludes to the fact that runaway slaves and criminals, once captured, were branded on the forehead with the letter "F" for **fugitivus**.

125   **privatarum rerum**: Refers to Catiline's personal wealth which he was mismanaging. Such mismanagement necessarily affected his reputation, **fama**, among Romans.
       libido: Catiline already was known for his sexual "desire." According to several sources, Catiline had been charged with corrupting a priestess of Vesta around 73 B.C.

[13] Quid est, Catilina? num dubitas id me imperante facere quod iam   119
tua sponte faciebas? Exire ex urbe iubet consul hostem. Interrogas me,   120
num in exsilium? Non iubeo, sed, si me consulis, suadeo. [VI] Quid est   121
enim, Catilina, quod te iam in hac urbe delectare possit? in qua nemo est   122
extra istam coniurationem perditorum hominum qui te non metuat, nemo   123
qui non oderit. Quae nota domesticae turpitudinis non inusta vitae tuae   124
est? quod privatarum rerum dedecus non haeret in fama? quae libido ab   125
oculis, quod facinus a manibus umquam tuis, quod flagitium a toto corpore   126
afuit? cui tu adulescentulo quem corruptelarum illecebris irretisses non   127
aut ad audaciam ferrum aut ad libidinem facem praetulisti? [14] Quid vero?   128
nuper cum morte superioris uxoris novis nuptiis locum vacuefecisses,   129
nonne etiam alio incredibili scelere hoc scelus cumulavisti? quod ego   130
praetermitto et facile patior sileri, ne in hac civitate tanti facinoris   131
immanitas aut exstitisse aut non vindicata esse videatur. Praetermitto   132
ruinas fortunarum tuarum quas omnis proximis Idibus tibi impendere   133
senties: ad illa venio quae non ad privatam ignominiam vitiorum tuorum,   134

127-28 **cui ... quem ... praetulisti**: **Cui adulescento** is a dative governed by the main verb
praetulisti, while the **quem** is a relative pronoun.
irretisses: "You would have ensnared." A subjunctive in a relative clause of characteristic.

128   **Quid vero?**: Calls attention to the following question.

129   **cum morte ... vacuefecisses**: **Cum** is a conjunction, while **morte** is an ablative of means.
superioris uxoris: In fact, Catiline's first wife.
novis nuptiis: "For a new marriage." Dative of purpose.

130   **nonne etiam**: "Why, you even ..., didn't you?"
incredibili scelere: Apparently Catiline killed his son from his first marriage in order to
please his second wife, Aurelia Orestilla.
Quod: = **et id**. Coordinating relative .

132   **Praetermitto**: A **praeteritio** which Cicero is using to slip in marginally relevant information
in an attempt to prove a point by innuendo rather than by evidence.

133   **omnis**: Accusative plural (cf. 17 and note) modifying **quas**, but translate as if it modified the
antecedent **ruinas**, i.e., **omnis ruinas quas**.
proximis Idibus: Ablative of time when. The **Kalendae** and the **Ides** were the standard
dates for loan repayments.

aio ais ait aiunt *def. v.* to say

assequor -i -secutus sum to accomplish, gain

comitium -i *n.* the Comitium (the meeting place in front of the Senate house)

conicio -ere -ieci -iectum to throw together, hurl

declinatio -onis *f.* a bending; sidestep

designatus/a/um (< designo) elect

difficultas -atis *f.* trouble, difficulty

effugio -ere -fugi -fugitum to escape, avoid

iucundus/a/um pleasant

obscurus/a/um covered, concealed

obsisto -ere obstiti obstitum *w/ dat.* to resist, thwart

omitto -ere -misi -missum to leave out, disregard

pertineo -ere -ui to pertain to

petitio -onis *f.* blow, attack

postea *adv.* later on, afterwards

princeps -cipis *m. subst.* leading man, chief

quot *indecl. adj.* how many

quotiens *exclamation* how often...!

salus -utis *f.* health, safety

spiritus -us *m.* breath, air

telum -i *n.* weapon, javelin

turpitudo -inis *f.* disgrace, shame

vito *1* to avoid, evade

---

135   **difficultatem**: "Financial straits."

135-36 **summam rem publicam**: "The highest interests of the state."

136   **vitam**: "Lives" (see note at 113).

138-41 **nesciat ... obstitisse**: **Nesciat** governs the following three infinitives (**stetisse, paravisse, obstitisse**) in indirect discourse. Cicero is alluding to the so-called "First Catilinarian Conspiracy." Although the ancient sources are confused and confusing, modern scholars agree that the unrest at the beginning of 65 B.C. was not an organized conspiracy. Catiline's role in this unrest is not clear. Cicero is again employing innuendo rather than fact to help build his case against Catiline.

138   **pridie Kalendas Ianuarias**: December 29, 66 B.C. Before the Julian calendar reform, all months had 29 days except for March, May, July, and October, all of which had 31.
Lepido et Tullo consulibus: This fixes the year as 66 B.C. The Romans marked years by the names of the consuls in an ablative absolute. A literal translation is "When Lepidus and Tullus were consuls," but for clarity begin your translation with "in the year ...."

139-40 **manum ... paravisse**: Repeat the **te** from 138 as the subject of the infinitive **paravisse**, while **manum** is the direct object.
consulum et principum ... causa: "For the sake of _verb_-ing the _noun_." Gerundive of purpose.

non ad domesticam tuam difficultatem ac turpitudinem, sed ad summam rem   135
publicam atque ad omnium nostrum vitam salutemque pertinent. [15] Potestne tibi   136
haec lux, Catilina, aut huius caeli spiritus esse iucundus, cum scias esse horum   137
neminem qui nesciat te pridie Kalendas Ianuarias Lepido et Tullo consulibus   138
stetisse in comitio cum telo, manum consulum et principum civitatis   139
interficiendorum causa paravisse, sceleri ac furori tuo non mentem aliquam aut   140
timorem tuum sed Fortunam populi Romani obstitisse?   141

Ac iam illa omitto — neque enim sunt aut obscura aut non multa commissa   142
postea — quotiens tu me designatum, quotiens vero consulem interficere conatus   143
es! quot ego tuas petitiones ita coniectas ut vitari posse non viderentur parva   144
quadam declinatione et, ut aiunt, corpore effugi! Nihil agis, nihil assequeris,   145

---

139   **in comitio cum telo**: It was a criminal offense to carry any kind of weapon within the city walls (**pomerium**) or, as here, onto the **Campus Martius** during an assembly (cf. 107-09).

142   **non multa**: "A few." A good example of **litotes** (two negatives making a vague positive for the sake of emphasis). The **neque** negates **sunt** and the **non** must be construed immediately before **multa** because of the parallelism set up by **aut ... aut**.

144-45 **petitiones ... effugi**: Cicero is using a fencing **metaphor** for how he escaped the attempts of Catiline. **Petitiones** are the thrusts, and the **parva quadam declinatione et ... corpore**, "with some little twist of the body," combine to mean a dodge or sidestep. By inserting **ut aiunt**, Cicero is in effect apologizing for his using the **metaphor**, as if such a figure were not appropriate for such an important political speech. Note the **hendiadys**, two nouns used to express one idea, found in **declinatione et ... corpore**.

144   **ita coniectas ut**: "Thrown together in such a way that ...." The result clause ends with **viderentur**.

adventus -us *m.* approach, arrival

assido -ere -sedi to sit down

casus -us *m.* chance, mishap

constituo -ere -stitui -stitutum to designate

consularis -e of consular rank, consular

contingo -ere -tigi -tactum *w/ dat.* to happen to

contumelia -ae *f.* reproach, insult

defigo -ere -fixi -fixum to plunge

desisto -ere -stiti -stitum to stop, cease

devoveo -ere -vovi -votum to devote, consecrate

elabor -i -lapsus sum to slip away, escape

excido -ere -cidi to fall out, fall

extorqueo -ere -torsi -tortum to wrest away, take by force

frequentia -ae *f.* crowd

inanis -e empty

initio *1* to initiate, consecrate

iudicium -i *n.* judgment, sentence

mehercule *interjection* by Hercules!

metuo -ere metui to fear, be afraid of

misericordia -ae *f.* compassion, pity

necessarius -i *m.* relative, client

necesse *indecl. adj. w/* esse to be necessary

nudus/a/um bare

odium -i *n.* hate, grudge

pacto (< pactum) *abl. sg.* in a way

paulo ante *adv.* a little while ago, shortly before

permoveo -ere -movi -motum to arouse

persaepe *adv.* very often

sica -ae *f.* dagger

simul atque *conj.* as soon as

subsellium -i *n.* seat, bench

taciturnitas -atis *f.* silence

tot *indecl. num. adj.* so many, in such numbers

vacuefacio -ere -feci -factum to make empty, vacate

---

146   **tibi**: Dative of reference ("your") with **manibus** (147).
de: "From."

147   **Quae quidem quibus**: Note the **alliteration**. The **quae** is again a coordinating relative (see 97 and note) and is the same as **et ea** with its antecedent being **sica**. **Quidem** is adverbial in force, meaning "indeed." The **quibus** introduces an indirect question after the verb **nescio** and agrees with **sacris**. In English word order, the sentence would read: **quidem nescio quibus sacris ea (sica) initiata ac devota sit abs te.**

148   **quod**: "That."
necesse ... esse: "It is necessary." Indirect discourse with **putas**.

151   **ut misericordia**: **Elliptical** for **ut misericordia permotus esse videar**. **Misericordia** is ablative. **quae ... nulla**: "None of which." By using **nulla** instead of **non** Cicero gives emphasis to the fact that Catiline deserves no pity at all.

153   **post**: "Within." An expression of time.

154   **vocis**: Translate as "spoken" with **contumeliam** (literally, "of the voice").

155-58 **Quid? ... putas?**: The two **quod** clauses are the subjects of **ferendum** (sc. **esse**) in 158. The main verb, then, is the **putas** of 158. There are (at least) two approaches to translation: (1) break up the three clauses into independent questions and translate the **Quid? quod** as "what of the fact that" and the following **quod** likewise; or (2) start by translating the main clause and then translate the **quod** clauses, i.e., "Then, with what disposition do you think you ought to bear the fact that ...."

neque tamen conari ac velle desistis. [16] Quotiens iam tibi extorta est ista sica de   146
manibus, quotiens excidit casu aliquo et elapsa est! Quae quidem quibus abs te   147
initiata sacris ac devota sit nescio, quod eam necesse putas esse in consulis   148
corpore defigere.   149

[VII] Nunc vero quae tua est ista vita? Sic enim iam tecum loquar, non ut odio   150
permotus esse videar, quo debeo, sed ut misericordia, quae tibi nulla debetur.   151
Venisti paulo ante in senatum: quis te ex hac tanta frequentia, tot ex tuis   152
amicis ac necessariis salutavit? Si hoc post hominum memoriam contigit nemini,   153
vocis exspectas contumeliam, cum sis gravissimo iudicio taciturnitatis oppressus?   154
Quid? quod adventu tuo ista subsellia vacuefacta sunt, quod omnes consulares,   155
qui tibi persaepe ad caedem constituti fuerunt, simul atque assedisti, partem   156
istam subselliorum nudam atque inanem reliquerunt, quo tandem animo tibi   157
ferendum putas?   158

[17] Servi mehercule mei si me isto pacto metuerent ut te metuunt omnes cives   159
tui, domum meam relinquendam putarem: tu tibi urbem non arbitraris? et si me   160

---

156   **tibi**: Dative of agent with a perfect passive participle, similar to the dative of agent with the
gerundive of obligation (passive periphrastic).
constituti fuerunt: This form is not in most grammar books since the usual perfect passive
is **constituti sunt**. Cicero may have liked the rhythm of this form better, but there is difference in meaning as well. The combination of perfect form of **esse** and perfect participle as a
predicate adjective emphasizes the completion of the action. In other words, Catiline desig-
nated certain Roman citizens for death many times already, but he failed to have them killed;
thus, he presumably no longer poses that sort of threat.

159-60 **cives tui**: "Your fellow citizens."

160   **relinquendam**: Sc. **esse**.
tibi: Dative of agent (cf. 156).
urbem: Sc. **relinquendam esse**.
non: = **nonne**; "surely you ..., don't you?"

agnosco -ere agnovi agnitum to recognize, acknowledge

aliquo *adv.* to somewhere, somewhere

aliquot *indecl. num. adj.* some, several

aspectus -us *m.* sight, view

careo -ere -ui *w/ abl.* to be without, go without

concedo -ere -cessi -cessum to retreat

conscientia -ae *f.* common knowledge

conspicio -ere -spexi -spectum to look at

direptio -onis *f.* plundering, pillaging

everto -ere -verti -versum to overthrow

exsisto -ere -stiti to appear

flagitium -i *n.* deed of shame, outrage, disgrace

impunitus/a/um unpunished, unchecked

infestus/a/um hostile, dangerous

iniuria *abl. sg.* wrongly, unjustly

iudico *1* to decide, judge

iustus/a/um just, right

malo malle malui *irr. v.* to prefer

nex necis *f.* murder

odi odisse *def. v. in perf. tenses only* to hate

offensus/a/um disliked, offensive

parricidium -i *n.* murder, parricide

placo *1* to soothe, appease

perfringo -ere -fregi -fractum to break down

pertimesco -ere -timui to become alarmed at, fear

praesentia -ae *f.* presence

quaestio -onis *f.* trial, court

ratio -onis *f.* way, manner

superiora (< **superior/superus**) *n. pl. subst.* the aforementioned, the foregoing

taceo -ere tacui tacitum to be silent, be quiet

valeo -ere valui valitum to be strong, be able; **valere ad** to succeed at

vereor -eri veritus sum to fear; respect

vexatio -onis *f.* harassing

---

161 **meis civibus**: This could either be a dative of reference ("for") or a dative of agent ("by") with the participle **suspectum**.

162 **quam**: "Rather than," because of the implied comparison in **mallem**.
conscientia: Ablative of means. To the Romans, **conscientia** did not imply the modern sense of "guilty conscience" so much as common knowledge.

164 **quorum ... eorum**: In English the antecedent usually precedes the pronoun, but in Latin the relative clause often precedes the antecedent. Translate the main clause first and then the relative clause.

166 **ab**: "Away from."
Nunc: "As it is now."

167-68 **te ... cogitare**: **Te** is the subject of **cogitare** in indirect statement.

168 **huius**: Refers back to **patria** (166). A common use of **hic haec hoc** is to connect two sentences and thus show that there is a common theme in both.

168-69 **verebere ... sequere**: Second person, future, deponent (see notes at 49 and 58).
verebere: "Respect" (< **vereor**).

---

meis civibus iniuria suspectum tam graviter atque offensum viderem, carere me   161

aspectu civium quam infestis omnium oculis conspici mallem: tu, cum conscientia   162

scelerum tuorum agnoscas odium omnium iustum et iam diu tibi debitum, dubitas   163

quorum mentes sensusque vulneras, eorum aspectum praesentiamque vitare?   164

Si te parentes timerent atque odissent tui neque eos ulla ratione placare posses,   165

ut opinor, ab eorum oculis aliquo concederes. Nunc te patria, quae communis   166

est parens omnium nostrum, odit ac metuit et iam diu nihil te iudicat nisi de   167

parricidio suo cogitare: huius tu neque auctoritatem verebere nec iudicium   168

sequere nec vim pertimesces?   169

   [18] Quae tecum, Catilina, sic agit et quodam modo tacita loquitur: "Nullum   170

iam aliquot annis facinus exstitit nisi per te, nullum flagitium sine te; tibi uni   171

multorum civium neces, tibi vexatio direptioque sociorum impunita fuit ac   172

libera; tu non solum ad neglegendas leges et quaestiones verum etiam ad   173

evertendas perfringendasque valuisti. Superiora illa, quamquam ferenda non   174

---

170   **Quae**: Coordinating = **et ea** (sc. **patria**). This lecture by the fatherland is a commonly cited example of **personification**. Note the **hyperbole** throughout the speech.
tecum ... agit: "Pleads with you." Notice how the general verb **agere** can come to mean many different things depending upon context.
quodam ... loquitur: **Oxymoron** (use of contradictory terms to describe the same concept). In other words, although silent, the fatherland somehow (**quodam modo**) is speaking. Cicero may also be playing on the silence of the senators themselves (cf. 154).

171   **annis**: Ablative of time within which.
tibi uni: "for you alone."

172   **neces ... direptioque**: **Neces** alludes to Catiline's involvement in the proscriptions of Sulla, 82 B.C.; **vexatio direptioque** refer to Catiline's propraetorship in Africa, 67 B.C., after which he was tried for extorting the province.

174-75 **ferenda ... fuerunt**: "Ought to have ...." The past tense of a passive periphrastic is similar in translation to **oportebat** (see note on 16).

abhorreo -ere -ui *w/ abl.* to be inconsistent with **ab** *w/ abl.*

adhibeo -ere -ui -itum to apply, use

aliquando *adv.* at some time

asservo *1* to watch over, keep under guard

audeo -ere ausus sum *semi-dep.* to be bold, dare

contineo -ere -ui -tentum to contain

custodia -ae *f.* guard, protection; house arrest

desino -ere -sii -situm to cease, stop

discedo -ere -cessi -cessum to depart, leave

fero ferre tuli latum to bear, tolerate

impetro *1* to prevail

increpo -are -crepui -crepitum to rattle, sound, make a noise

ineo -ire -ii -itum to enter into; to attempt

moenia -ium *n. pl.* ramparts, walls of a city

paries parietis *m.* wall (of a house)

quia *conj.* since, because

recipio -ere -cepi -ceptum to receive; welcome

repudio *1* to reject, refuse

sin *conj.* but if

sodalis -is *m./f.* companion, friend, pal

tuto *adv.* safely, safe

verus/a/um well-founded, justifiable

---

175 **ut potui**: "As best I could."
nunc vero: "But now." The **nunc** indicates that the fatherland is returning to the present situation, and the **vero** emphasizes the difference between now and the previous times.

177 **ferendum**: Singular because of the collective notion expressed in its subjects, the previous infinitives, **esse**, **timeri**, and **videri** (in 175-76). Accordingly, the infinitives are gerunds. **Quam ob rem**: "And for this reason," "therefore." **Quam** is a coordinating relative (see note at 97).

178 **mihi**: "From me." The dative of separation ("from") is used with a person instead of the ablative, the case which would be expected to indicate separation. This use of the dative is an extension of the dative of reference. In other words, to the Roman mind the dative is the more personal expression of interest in the action of the verb than the ablative.
verus ... falsus: Both modify an implied **timor**.

178-79 **ne opprimar ... ut ... desinam**: Both purpose clauses depend upon the main verb, **eripe**.

180 **nonne ... debeat**: "It (the fatherland) would need ..., wouldn't it?"

181 **Quid**: "What of the fact ...." Translate the following **quod** and the one in 182 as "that."
in custodiam: The full legal phrase is **in custodiam liberam**. Roman citizens of rank were put under house arrest with another citizen taking responsibility for guarding the accused citizen.

---

fuerunt, tamen ut potui tuli; nunc vero me totam esse in metu propter unum te,   175

quicquid increpuerit, Catilinam timeri, nullum videri contra me consilium iniri   176

posse quod a tuo scelere abhorreat, non est ferendum. Quam ob rem discede   177

atque hunc mihi timorem eripe; si est verus, ne opprimar, sin falsus, ut tandem   178

aliquando timere desinam."   179

[VIII] [19] Haec si tecum, ut dixi, patria loquatur, nonne impetrare debeat,   180

etiam si vim adhibere non possit? Quid quod tu te in custodiam dedisti,   181

quod vitandae suspicionis causa ad M'. Lepidum te habitare velle dixisti? A quo   182

non receptus etiam ad me venire ausus es, atque ut domi meae te asservarem   183

rogasti. Cum a me quoque id responsum tulisses, me nullo modo posse isdem   184

parietibus tuto esse tecum, quia magno in periculo essem quod isdem moenibus   185

contineremur, ad Q. Metellum praetorem venisti. A quo repudiatus ad sodalem   186

---

182   **ad**: = **apud**.
       M'.: = **Manium**.

183   **ut ... asservarem**: Jussive noun clause (indirect command) after **rogasti** (184).

184   **rogasti**: = **rogavisti (syncopation)**.
       id responsum: "The same answer, that ...." This answer is elaborated by the following accusative, **me**, and infinitive, **esse** (185).

184-85 **isdem parietibus**: "Within the same walls." Ablative of instrument, but best translated as if locative.

185-86 **quia ... essem ... contineremur**: A clause subordinate to any words or ideas expressed in indirect statement (accusative with infinitive) will usually have a subjunctive verb. Translate as if the verb were indicative.

185   **moenibus**: Note the contrast here between **moenibus**, "walls of the city," and **parietibus**, "walls of a house."

abeo -ire -ii -itum to go away, depart

abhorreo -ere -ui *w/ abl.* to be inconsistent with _ab w/ abl._

animadverto -ere -verti -versum to notice

attendo -ere attendi attentum to pay attention to

auctoritas -atis *f.* lead; sign

carcer -eris *m.* cell, prison

custodio -ire -ivi -itum to guard, watch over

demigro *1* to depart, leave

dignus/a/um *w/ abl.* worthy of

diligens -ntis careful, attentive

dubito *1* to hesitate

ecquis ecquid anyone, anything; any _noun_ at all

egredior -i -gressus sum to go out, leave, depart

emorior -i -mortuus sum to die off, die

fore = futurum esse

fuga -ae *f.* flight, escape

iustus/a/um right, just

loquentium *pres. participle* < loquor

mando *1* to hand over, entrust

mos moris *m.* habit, custom; *pl.* character, practice

obtempero *1* to comply, obey

quam *w/ adj./adv.* how _adj./adv._

referre *in the phrase* ad senatum referre to present before the Senate for debate

sagax -acis keen, quick, shrewd

silentium -i *n.* silence

solitudo -inis *f.* loneliness; lonely place, wilderness

supplicium -i *n.* punishment

suspicor *1* mistrust, suspect

videlicet *adv.* obviously, namely, of course

vinculum -i *n.* chain

vindico *1* to punish

voluntas -atis *f.* will, desire

---

187   **virum optimum ... videlicet**: With strong **irony**. In fact, being in the custody of Marcus Metellus allowed Catiline to attend secret meetings with his co-conspirators.
demigrasti: = **demigravisti** (**syncopation**).

189   **videtur**: The subject is the "he" implied by the following **qui**. Latin tends to personalize subjects that are normally impersonal in English constructions. In translation **videtur debere** becomes "does it seem right," or "does it seem that one ought." Translate the sentence as if the word order were **sed quam longe a carcere atque a vinculis videtur debere abesse (ei), qui se ipse iam dignum custodia iudicarit.**

190   **iudicarit**: = **iudicaverit** (**syncopation**). A perfect subjunctive in a relative claue of characteristic.

191   **aequo animo**: "With resignation." Ablative of manner.

191-92 **in aliquas terras**: Freely translated, "anywhere else but here." The indefinite pronoun **aliquas** suggests that Cicero is not thinking of a specific place so much as that Catiline not be in Rome.

192   **multis ... debitisque**: Ablatives of separation with **ereptam**.

194   **Refer ... ad senatum**: Sc. **rem**. **Referre rem ad senatum** was the standard idiom for "to bring up a matter before the Senate for debate or consideration." There is a legal problem here: only the courts could pronounce the sentence of exile. Catiline says (**dicis**, 195) that he will obey whatever the Senate decides, knowing full well that the Senate had no real jurisdiction.

tuum, virum optimum, M. Metellum demigrasti, quem tu videlicet et ad   187

custodiendum te diligentissimum et ad suspicandum sagacissimum et ad   188

vindicandum fortissimum fore putasti. Sed quam longe videtur a carcere   189

atque a vinculis abesse debere qui se ipse iam dignum custodia iudicarit?   190

[20] Quae cum ita sint, Catilina, dubitas, si emori aequo animo non potes, abire in   191

aliquas terras et vitam istam multis suppliciis iustis debitisque ereptam fugae   192

solitudinique mandare?   193

"Refer" inquis "ad senatum"; id enim postulas et, si hic ordo placere sibi   194

decreverit te ire in exsilium, obtemperaturum te esse dicis. Non referam, id quod   195

abhorret a meis moribus, et tamen faciam ut intellegas quid hi de te sentiant.   196

Egredere ex urbe, Catilina, libera rem publicam metu, in exsilium, si hanc vocem   197

exspectas, proficiscere.   198

Quid est? ecquid attendis, ecquid animadvertis horum silentium? Patiuntur,   199

tacent. Quid exspectas auctoritatem loquentium, quorum voluntatem tacitorum   200

---

194   **placere sibi**: = **se cupere**.

195   **dicis**: That is, Catiline has been baiting the senators.

195-96 **Non referam ... moribus**: Cicero refuses, however, to put the matter before the Senate
perhaps not on the grounds that it is illegal, but because to do so would be too harsh (**id quod
abhorret a meis moribus**) given the current animosity towards Catiline. Cicero is playing
the crowd here. By using false restraint he attempts to create greater resolve among the
senators.

196   **faciam ut intellegas**: "I will make you understand ...." Literally, "I will make it so that you
understand."

197   **vocem**: = **verbum**, i.e., **exsilium**. A **metonymy**.

200   **Quid**: = **cur**.
tacitorum: "Although silent." Cicero is echoing the introduction to the **personification** of
the fatherland at 170. Cicero is equating, now for perhaps the second time (cf. 154 and note
at 170), the Senate's silence with a call to action. Note the building emotional pitch in 199-
210, a **crescendo** and **climax** which begins with these rhetorical questions.

adduco -ere -duxi -ductum to prompt, induce

adulescens -ntis *m./f.* young (man), a youth

auctoritas -atis *f.* support, approval

circumsto -are -steti to surround, threaten

contineo -ere -tenui -tentum to restrain, hold in check

corrigo -ere -rexi -rectum to straighten out, fix

duint (< **do**) *archaic pres. subjunctive* to give, grant

eques equitis *m.* knight, member of equestrian order

exaudio -ire -ivi -itum to hear clearly, perceive

frango -ere fregi fractum to break, destroy

frequentia -ae *f.* crowd

honestus/a/um worthy, honorable

impendeo -ere *def. v. w/ dat.* to threaten

induco -ere -duxi -ductum to bring; persuade; **animum inducere** to decide

infero -ferre -tuli illatum to bring <u>acc.</u> against <u>dat.</u>

invidia -ae *f.* envy, ill will

meditor *1* to contemplate, consider

perspicio -ere -spexi -spectum to see plainly, observe

posteritas -atis *f.* the future

probo *1* to approve, recommend

prosequor -i -secutus sum to pursue; escort

quiesco -ere quievi quietum to keep still, take no action

studeo -ere -ui *w/ dat.* to be eager for

studium -i *n.* eagerness, zeal

tametsi *conj.* and yet

tempestas -atis *f.* storm

usque *adv.* all the way

utinam *adv.* would that, oh that

videlicet *adv.* clearly, obviously

vilis -e cheap; poor

201-02 **si ... dixissem**: Repeat the **dixissem** for both **si** clauses.

202-03 **mihi ... intulisset**: **Senatus** is the subject of **intulisset**; **vim** and **manus** are direct objects; **mihi consuli** is the indirect object.

203 **vim et manus**: "Violent hands." **Hendiadys** (cf. 77).

203-04 **cum ...**: "When ...." These **cum** clauses take the indicative mood since they are explanatory clauses. The main verb defines the meaning of the action in each **cum** clause. Note the **juxtapositions** and **antitheses**.

205 **auctoritas**: This abstract noun has many meanings depending upon its context. In 200, it meant "lead," but here it must mean "support." All of its definitions, however seemingly divergent in English, come from the root **-aug-** which means "increase" or "nourish."

206 **ceterique fortissimi cives**: "And the rest of the bravest citizens." Cicero, here referring to the middle class below the **equites**, is careful to include as many people as possible who may be threatened by and stand in opposition to Catiline.

207-08 **quorum ... potuisti**: The doors of the temple were left open during meetings to allow the regular citizenry to overhear the proceedings. Cicero is referring to the noises the crowd outside made during his accusations.

209-10 **ut ... prosequantur**: Indirect command (jussive noun clause) patterning with **adducam**.
te ... relinquentem: **Relinquentem** modifies **te** and indicates the end of the participial phrase (cf. 19-20 and note); **haec** is the object of **relinquentem**.

---

perspicis? [21] At si hoc idem huic adulescenti optimo P. Sestio, si fortissimo   201
viro M. Marcello dixissem, iam mihi consuli hoc ipso in templo senatus   202
iure optimo vim et manus intulisset. De te autem, Catilina, cum quiescunt,   203
probant, cum patiuntur, decernunt, cum tacent, clamant, neque hi solum   204
quorum tibi auctoritas est videlicet cara, vita vilissima, sed etiam illi equites   205
Romani, honestissimi atque optimi viri, ceterique fortissimi cives qui   206
circumstant senatum, quorum tu et frequentiam videre et studia perspicere   207
et voces paulo ante exaudire potuisti. Quorum ego vix abs te iam diu   208
manus ac tela contineo, eosdem facile adducam ut te haec quae vastare   209
iam pridem studes relinquentem usque ad portas prosequantur.   210
[IX] [22] Quamquam quid loquor? te ut ulla res frangat, tu ut umquam te corrigas,   211
tu ut ullam fugam meditere, tu ut ullum exsilium cogites? Utinam tibi istam   212
mentem di immortales duint! tametsi video, si mea voce perterritus ire in exsilium   213
animum induxeris, quanta tempestas invidiae nobis, si minus in praesens tempus   214
recenti memoria scelerum tuorum, at in posteritatem impendeat. Sed est tanti,   215

---

211   **Quamquam**: "And yet."
   quid: = **cur**.
   loquor: Cicero is the only one speaking (cf. 154, 170, 200 and notes); but here, as his argument reaches its **climax**, he implicitly agrees with the "silent treatment." One may imagine Catiline acted innocent as Cicero explained the situation to him. Cicero now sees no point in reasoning with him.

211-12 **ut ... cogites**: "As if ... could." Here **ut** is used four times as an interrogative particle introducing **ironic rhetorical questions**. **Ut** with a subjunctive verb often introduces questions of surprise or indignation. Accordingly, the **anaphora**, **asyndeton**, and **rhetorical questions** reinforce Cicero's exaspiration and contempt.

212   **meditere**: Second person, present, deponent, subjunctive. For form, see note at 58.

212-13 **Utinam ... duint**: "If only ...." **Utinam** with the present subjunctive is the normal form for expressing a wish. Cicero here, however, also preserves the archaic form **duint** (instead of the expected **dent**), perhaps because the archaic forms of the subjunctive were often used in prayers and curses.

214   **nobis**: Dative governed by **impendeat** (215). Translate as if **mihi**.

215   **recenti memoria**: "Because of ...." Ablative of cause.
   at: "At least." Parallel to **si minus** (214).

215-16 **Sed est tanti, dum modo ...**: "But it (the risk of unpopularity) is worth it so long as ...."
   Tanti is a genitive of value.

alienus -i *m.* stranger, foreigner

cedo cedere cessi cessum *w/ dat.* to yield to, give in to

concito *1* to stir up, excite

conferre se to betake oneself, go

dum modo *conj.* so long as, provided that

eicio -ere -ieci -iectum to throw out, banish

exsulto *1 w/ dat.* to revel in, delight in

furor -is *m.* madness, insanity

impius/a/um undutiful; wicked, shameless

importunus/a/um dangerous, cruel

infero -ferre intuli illatum to bring <u>acc.</u> against <u>dat.</u> ;
    bellum inferre to wage war on <u>dat.</u>

invidiam conflare to arouse animosity towards <u>dat.</u>

invito *1* to invite, ask

isse *perf. inf.* < **eo ire**

iussu (< **iussus**) *abl. sg.* by order

latrocinium -i *n.* robbery, piracy

laus laudis *f.* praise

malo malle malui *irr. v.* to prefer

manus -us *f.* band, gang

metus -us *m.* fear, dread

moles -is *f.* mass, burden

pergo -ere perrexi perrectum to keep on, proceed

perditus/a/um (< **perdo**) corrupt, depraved

postulo *1* to demand

praedico *1* to claim

privatus/a/um personal

pudor -oris *m.* shame, decency

ratio -onis *f.* reason, thought

recta *adv.* straight, directly

sceleratus/a/um wicked, criminal

secerno -ere -crevi -cretum to separate, set apart

seiungo -ere -iunxi -iunctum to separate, sever

sermo -onis *m.* talk, conversation

servio -ire -ivi itum *w/ dat.* to serve

sin *conj.* but if, if on the contrary

sustineo -ere -ui -tentum to endure, withstand

turpitudo -inis *f.* disgrace, shame

vitium -i *n.* crime, vice

---

217   **commoveare**: Second person, present, passive, subjunctive (see note at 58).
        temporibus: "Critical situation."

218   **est postulandum**: Translate as an impersonal verb governing the three noun (**ut**) clauses that
        precede.
        is: "Such a one that ...." Here, **is** signals a result clause as **talis** or **tantus** commonly do.

220   **Quam ob rem**: "Therefore" (cf. 177 and note).

220-21 **mihi inimico ... tuo**: Dative with **conflare invidiam**. With **inimico** Cicero is giving
        Catiline's version of the plot; hence **ut praedicas**. As the following sentence affirms, Cicero
        may have been nervous about the public's likely perception that Catiline was an **inimicus**
        rather than a **hostis** (cf. **hostem** in 120 and note); he speaks with strong **irony** here and in the
        following sentence.

223   **mavis**: Present indicative of **malo**.

dum modo tua ista sit privata calamitas et a rei publicae periculis seiungatur.   216

Sed tu ut vitiis tuis commoveare, ut legum poenas pertimescas, ut temporibus   217

rei publicae cedas non est postulandum. Neque enim is es, Catilina, ut te aut   218

pudor a turpitudine aut metus a periculo aut ratio a furore revocarit.   219

      [23] Quam ob rem, ut saepe iam dixi, proficiscere ac, si mihi inimico, ut praedicas,   220

tuo conflare vis invidiam, recta perge in exsilium; vix feram sermones hominum,   221

si id feceris; vix molem istius invidiae, si in exsilium iussu consulis iveris, sustinebo.   222

Sin autem servire meae laudi et gloriae mavis, egredere cum importuna   223

sceleratorum manu, confer te ad Manlium, concita perditos cives, secerne te a   224

bonis, infer patriae bellum, exsulta impio latrocinio, ut a me non eiectus ad   225

alienos, sed invitatus ad tuos isse videaris.   226

223-26 **Sin ... videaris**: Six imperative verbs, surrounded by two subordinate clauses. The impera-
tives build up to the end of the **period**, a figure known as **climax**. Notice that Cicero begins
by introducing Catiline's side of the story, and then, in a rhetorical flourish, dismisses the
possibility without logical argument.

225   **impio latrocinio**: A treasonable offense implying Catiline is indeed a public enemy. In 63
B.C., Pompey was still in the eastern Mediterranean cleaning up the problem with pirates.
The Romans were keenly aware of the threat posed by **latrocinium**.

225-26 **ut ... non eiectus ... videaris**: This may either be purpose or result since **non** modifies
eiectus, not the verb **videaris**. Remember that a negative result is never introduced by **ne**,
but rather **ut ... non**.

affero -ferre attuli allatum to bring to

altaria -ium *n. pl.* altar

amentia -ae *f.* madness, folly

aquila -ae *f.* eagle (and by **synecdoche** the whole legionary standard or pole on which a metal eagle was placed)

armati -orum *m. pl. subst.* armed men

careo -ere -ui *w/ abl.* to be without, go without

confido -ere -fisus sum *semi-dep.* to trust, be confident

constituo -ere -stitui -stitutum (*in line 228*) to decide, designate; (*in line 231*) set up

dextra *and* **dextera -ae** *subst. f.* the right hand

dolor -is *m.* pain, suffering

effrenatus/a/um unbridled, unrestrained

exerceo -ere -ercui -ercitum *trans. v.* to practice, train

Forum Aurelium -i *n.* Forum Aurelium (a small market town in Etruria about 75 miles north of Rome on the Via Aurelia)

funestus/a/um fatal; mournful

furiosus/a/um mad, insane

invito *1* to invite, ask

nefarius/a/um unspeakable, wicked

nex necis *f.* slaughter, murder

pango -ere pepigi pactum to arrange, agree upon

pario -ere peperi partum to produce

perniciosus/a/um *w/ dat.* destructive to

praemitto -ere -misi -missum to send forward, dispatch in advance

praestolor *1 w/ dat.* to wait for, expect

sacrarium -i *n.* shrine

transferro -ferre -tuli -latum to carry <u>acc.</u> across, pass <u>acc.</u> over

veneror *1* to worship; pay homage to

voluntas -atis *f.* will, wish

227-31 This **periodic sentence** breaks down into a series of shorter clauses:

    Quamquam quid ego te invitem

        (te) a quo iam sciam esse praemissos

            (eos) qui tibi ad Forum Aurelium praestolarentur armati

        (te) cui sciam pactam et constitutam cum Manlio diem

        (te) a quo etiam aquilam illam argenteam

            (aquilam) quam tibi ac tuis omnibus confido perniciosam ac funestam futuram (esse)

            (aquilam) cui domi tuae sacrarium scelerum constitutum fuit

    sciam esse praemissam?

227   **Quamquam**: "And yet" (cf. 211).

       quid: = **cur**.

       sciam: Subjunctive by attraction to the deliberative subjunctive **invitem**.

227-28 **qui ... praestolarentur armati**: "In order that they ...." Relative clause of purpose, subordinate to **sciam**.

228   **cui**: "By whom." This relative is subordinate to **invitem** in 227. The relative **cui** is a dative of agent with the perfect passive participle **constitutam**.

229   **diem**: Note that **diem** is feminine here (rather than the usual masculine) because this is a special day.

       aquilam: This is the standard which was supposed to have belonged to Marius. Thus it becomes a symbol for Catiline's leadership of the **popularis** cause.

       tibi ac tuis omnibus: Datives patterning with **perniciosam** (230).

[24] Quamquam quid ego te invitem, a quo iam sciam esse praemissos qui tibi 227

ad Forum Aurelium praestolarentur armati, cui sciam pactam et constitutam 228

cum Manlio diem, a quo etiam aquilam illam argenteam quam tibi ac tuis omnibus 229

confido perniciosam ac funestam futuram, cui domi tuae sacrarium scelerum 230

constitutum fuit, sciam esse praemissam? Tu ut illa carere diutius possis, quam 231

venerari ad caedem proficiscens solebas, a cuius altaribus saepe istam impiam 232

dexteram ad necem civium transtulisti? 233

[X] [25] Ibis tandem aliquando quo te iam pridem tua ista cupiditas effrenata ac 234

furiosa rapiebat; neque enim tibi haec res affert dolorem, sed quandam 235

incredibilem voluptatem. Ad hanc te amentiam natura peperit, voluntas exercuit, 236

fortuna servavit. Numquam tu non modo otium sed ne bellum quidem nisi nefarium 237

---

230 **futuram**: Sc. **esse**.
    cui: Dative indirect object of **constitutum fuit** (231). The antecedent is **aquilam** (229).

231 **constitutum fuit**: For form, see note at 156.
    sciam esse praemissam: For emphasis, Cicero has delayed the main verb of the relative clause (introduced by **a quo**, 229) until the very end. Remember the basic rule that embedded clauses (clauses within other clauses) must finish before the previous clause may continue (cf. note at 47-48).
    ut ... possis: Another question of indignation (or scorn — cf. 211 and note at 211-12) which implies, with bitter irony, that Catiline could never be far away from his prized standard. Military standards in ancient Rome were in fact closely protected by legions, and for a legion to lose its standard in battle was the highest disgrace for all soldiers of the legion and Rome itself.

234-35 **iam pridem ... rapiebat**: "Had been hurling for a long time ...." The **iam pridem** indicates that the action of the verb has been taking place all the way up to the time of the tense of that verb. Thus the imperfect **rapiebat** translates with the normally pluperfect "had" and the English present participle to indicate ongoing motion. (Cf. **iam pridem** with the present tense in 117 and note.)

236-37 **natura ... servavit**: **Tricolon** and **climax**.

237 **Numquam tu non modo ... sed ne ... quidem**: "Not only have you never ... but not even ...." The thought is that Catiline would outright reject any desire for peace, and then he would further only want to wage the most heinous war. Note the **alliteration**.

---

bacchor *1* to revel, exult

bona -orum *n. pl. subst.* goods, property

concupisco -cupiscere -cupivi -cupitum to long for, desire

confectus/a/um (< **conficio**) weakened

conflo *1* to blow together, throw together

consulatus -us *m.* consulship

deprecor *1* to pray to avert; plead against

derelinquo -ere -liqui -lictum to abandon

detestor *1* to curse, denounce

etenim *conj.* and indeed, and really

exsul -is *m./f.* exile

exsulto *1 w/ dat.* to revel in, delight in

fames -is *f.* hunger, starvation; want, famine

frigus -oris *n.* cold, chill

gaudium -i *n.* gladness, enjoyment

humi (< **humus**) *loc.* on the ground

improbus/a/um wicked, base

insidior *1 w/ dat.* to lie in wait for, plot against

laetitia -ae *f.* joy, delight

mando *1* to hand over, entrust

maritus -i *m.* husband

meditor *1* to contemplate

nanciscor -i nactus sum to obtain

nomino *1* to name, call

obeo -ire -ii -itum *w/ dat.* to meet, go up to

obsideo -ere -sedi -sessum *w/ dat.* to lie in wait for

ostento *1* to show, display

otiosi *m. pl. subst.* the neutral ones, the idle

patientia -ae *f.* endurance

penitus *adv.* deeply

percipio -ere -cepi ceptum to observe, learn

perfruor -i -fructus *w/ abl.* to enjoy fully, be greatly delighted with

potius...quam *conj.* rather than

proficio -ere -feci -fectum to accomplish

querimonia -ae *f.* complaint, lament

repello -ere -ppuli -pulsum to drive <u>acc.</u> back from <u>abl.</u>

somnus -i *m.* sleep

stuprum -i *n.* debauchery, lewdness

suscipio -ere -cepi -ceptum to undertake, attempt

vigilo *1* to stay awake; be watchful

voluptas -atis *f.* pleasure, delight

238-39 **Nactus ... manum**: Cicero embeds one prepositional phrase within another; in English word order:

> Nactus es manum improborum conflatam
>> ex perditis atque derelictis
>> ab omni non modo fortuna verum etiam spe.

ab: "By." **Personification** because **ab** is usually used with "personal" agents. Normally an object or concept performing or causing action stands by itself in the ablative.

240　**Hic**: "Here," i.e., among his gang of the worst people.

241　**neque ... quemquam**: "Not even one" (see note at 47).

242　**Ad huius vitae studium**: "For the pursuit of this lifestyle."
meditati ... sunt: "Were contemplated." Here the deponent verb really is passive with the subject **illi ... labores tui**.
feruntur: "Are much talked about."
labores: "Hardships." The hardships are detailed by the infinitives **iacere** (243) and **vigilare** (244).

concupisti. Nactus es ex perditis atque ab omni non modo fortuna verum etiam   238
spe derelictis conflatam improborum manum.   239

[26] Hic tu qua laetitia perfruere, quibus gaudiis exsultabis, quanta in voluptate   240
bacchabere, cum in tanto numero tuorum neque audies virum bonum quemquam   241
neque videbis! Ad huius vitae studium meditati illi sunt qui feruntur labores tui,   242
iacere humi non solum ad obsidendum stuprum verum etiam ad facinus   243
obeundum, vigilare non solum insidiantem somno maritorum verum etiam bonis   244
otiosorum. Habes ubi ostentes tuam illam praeclaram patientiam famis, frigoris,   245
inopiae rerum omnium, quibus te brevi tempore confectum esse senties. [27] Tantum   246
profeci, cum te a consulatu reppuli, ut exsul potius temptare quam consul vexare   247
rem publicam posses, atque ut id quod esset a te scelerate susceptum latrocinium   248
potius quam bellum nominaretur.   249

[XI] Nunc, ut a me, patres conscripti, quandam prope iustam patriae   250
querimoniam detester ac deprecer, percipite, quaeso, diligenter quae dicam, et   251
ea penitus animis vestris mentibusque mandate. Etenim si mecum patria, quae   252
mihi vita mea multo est carior, si cuncta Italia, si omnis res publica loquatur: 253

---

245   **Habes ubi ostentes**: "You have the opportunity to show ...."

246   **Tantum**: "Just this much."

247-49 **ut ... posses ... ut ... nominaretur**: Substantive noun clauses explaining what Cicero means
by the **tantum** (246).

247   **reppuli**: **Repellere** was the standard verb meaning "to defeat" in the context of an election.
exsul ... consul: Note the **alliteration** and **antithesis**.

250   **a me**: Ablative of separation with **detester** and **deprecer** (251).

251   **quae**: "The things which." The antecedent of **quae** is expressed in the next clause by the **ea** (252).
dicam: Future indicative.

252   **patria**: = **Roma**.

252-53 **si mecum ... si cuncta ... si omnis**: Another **anaphora** (cf. 6-8).

an *conj. (between two questions)* Or ...? Or is it that ...?

auctor -is *m.* promoter, leader

cognosco -ere -novi -nitum to learn; *perf.* know

commendatio -onis *f.* recommendation

comperio -ire -peri -pertum to find out, learn

deficio -ere -feci -fectum to defect, abandon

effero -ferre extuli elatum to raise

evocator -is *m.* recruiter

exspecto *1* to wait for

gradus -us *m.* step

gratiam referre to return a favor

immitto -ere -misi -missum to send against

impedio -ire -pedivi -peditum to hinder, prevent

invidia -ae *f.* unpopularity

macto *1* to put to death, kill

maiores -um *m. pl. subst.* ancestors

mature *adv.* promptly, at the right time

mos maiorum traditions of the ancestors, customs

multo *1* to punish

perditus/a/um (< **perdo**) corrupt

persaepe *adv.* very often

posteritas -atis *f.* the future; future generations

praeclarus/a/um distinguished, famous

rogo *1* to ask; *of laws* to pass

supplicium -i *n.* punishment, penalty

tune = tu-ne

vinculum -i *n.* bond, chain

254-58 **Tune ... videatur?**: Again, the **period** breaks down into several short clauses and phrases:

> Tune eum
>> quem esse hostem comperisti
>> quem ducem belli futurum vides
>> quem exspectari imperatorem in castris hostium sentis
>>> auctorem sceleris,
>>> principem coniurationis,
>>> evocatorem servorum et civium perditorum,
>
> exire patiere
>> ut abs te non emissus ex urbe, sed immissus in urbem esse videatur?

255   **futurum**: = **futurum esse**.

256-57 **evocatorem ... perditorum**: Sallust reports that Catiline refused the help of slaves, but that one of his advisers encouraged their recruitment. Cicero takes rhetorical advantage of the fact that the Romans still remember acutely the slave revolt of Spartacus less than ten years earlier (73-71 B.C.); and, no doubt, the Romans were also aware of the current slave uprising in Apulia and at Capua, the capital of Campania southeast of Rome.

258-59 **Nonne ... imperabis**: Notice here and above how the fatherland likes to speak in groups of three. This figure is called **tricolon**. Also, note the gradual building of successive phrases, **climax**.

"M. Tulli, quid agis? Tune eum quem esse hostem comperisti, quem ducem   254
belli futurum vides, quem exspectari imperatorem in castris hostium sentis,   255
auctorem sceleris, principem coniurationis, evocatorem servorum et civium   256
perditorum, exire patiere, ut abs te non emissus ex urbe, sed immissus in urbem   257
esse videatur? Nonne hunc in vincula duci, non ad mortem rapi, non summo   258
supplicio mactari imperabis? Quid tandem te impedit? mosne maiorum? [28] At   259
persaepe etiam privati in hac re publica perniciosos cives morte multarunt. An   260
leges quae de civium Romanorum supplicio rogatae sunt? At numquam in hac   261
urbe qui a re publica defecerunt civium iura tenuerunt.   262

"An invidiam posteritatis times? Praeclaram vero populo Romano refers gratiam,   263
qui te, hominem per te cognitum, nulla commendatione maiorum, tam mature ad   264
summum imperium per omnis honorum gradus extulit, si propter invidiam aut   265

---

260   **persaepe**: A bit **hyperbolic**. In fact, Cicero has only been able to muster about three ex-
        amples — and not all exact precedents at that (see 17-22 and 28-34).

261   **leges**: Cicero is probably referring to the **Lex Valeria** (508 B.C.), which granted Roman
        citizens an appeal to the assembly before a sentence was carried out; and the **Lex Porcia**
        (probably 197 B.C.), which allowed a Roman citizen to go into exile to avoid scourging or
        the death penalty and asserted the rite of appeal. Then Gaius Gracchus reasserted the right to
        appeal in 123 B.C. with the proposed **Lex Sempronia**. The bottom line, however, was that
        there was a fundamental conflict between the **Lex Sempronia** and the **senatus consultum
        ultimum** (see 28-36 and notes).

264   **hominem ... maiorum**: Cicero was a **novus homo** and here emphasizes that he has
        achieved everything on his own, without the benefit of an established family.
        tam mature: Cicero was elected **suo anno** ("in his own year"), i.e., the first year he was
        eligible to be elected to an office.

265   **omnis**: Accusative plural modifying **gradus** (cf. 17 and note).
        honorum gradus: I.e., the **cursus honorum**, the normal sequence of offices leading up to
        the consulship.

ardeo -ere arsi arsum to be on fire, burn

complures -ia several, many

conflagro *1* to burn up, be consumed

contamino *1* to pollute, stain

existimo *1* to estimate, judge

factu (< **facio**) *supine* "to do"

Flaccus -i *m.* Flaccus

fortitudo -inis *f.* bravery

gladiator -is *m.* gladiator; thug

Gracchi -orum *m. pl.* the Gracchi brothers

honesto *1* to dignify, honor, adorn

hora -ae *f.* hour, time

impendeo -ere *def. v. w/ dat.* to overhang, threaten

incendium -i *n.* fire; *pl.* arson

inertia -ae *f.* laziness

interficio -ere -feci -fectum to kill, murder

iudico *1* to judge, decide

multo *1* to punish

neglego -ere -lexi -lectum to disregard, neglect

nequitia -ae *f.* worthlessness

pario -ere peperi partum to acquire, get

parricida -ae *m.* assassin, parricide

redundo *1 w/ dat.* to wash back over; overwhelm

sanctus/a/um consecrated, inviolable

sanguis -inis *m.* blood

Saturninus -i *m.* Saturninus

severitas -atis *f.* seriousness, sternness

superior -ius (< **superus**) *comp. adj.* before, previous

tecta -orum *n. pl.* houses, homes

vasto *1* to lay waste, destroy

vehementius *comp. adv.* more strongly, more forcefully

vexo *1* to harass

---

266   **quis**: "Any," modifying **metus** (267). Sc. **tibi** (dative of possession) "you have...."

267   **vehementius ... quam**: An **ellipsis**. Cicero is comparing two types of unpopularity, one from overreaction, the other from indolence. The genitives — **fortitudinis**, **inertiae**, and **nequitiae** (268) — give the source of the **invidia**.

268-69 **cum ... ardebunt**: Cicero runs together the successive verbs without conjunctions, an **asyndeton**.
        vexabuntur urbes, tecta ardebunt: **Chiasmus**.

270-71 **vocibus ... mentibus**: **Antithesis**. The **vocibus** are the words just spoken by the fatherland, while the **mentibus** are the unspoken thoughts of the senators.

271-73 **iudicarem ... non dedissem**: "... I were (now) judging ... I would not have given ...." A mixed conditional. By putting the main verb's tense in the past time, Cicero is emphasizing the fact that he would have killed Catiline the very moment he thought it appropriate.

271   **factu**: "To do." An ablative supine, best translated by the English infinitive. The ablative supine is a verbal extension of the ablative of description.

272   **Catilinam morte multari**: In apposition to **hoc optimum factu** (271).

alicuius periculi metum salutem civium tuorum neglegis. [29] Sed si quis est invidiae   266

metus, non est vehementius severitatis ac fortitudinis invidia quam inertiae ac   267

nequitiae pertimescenda. An, cum bello vastabitur Italia, vexabuntur urbes,   268

tecta ardebunt, tum te non existimas invidiae incendio conflagraturum?"   269

[XII] His ego sanctissimis rei publicae vocibus et eorum hominum qui hoc idem   270

sentiunt mentibus pauca respondebo. Ego, si hoc optimum factu iudicarem,   271

patres conscripti, Catilinam morte multari, unius usuram horae gladiatori isti   272

ad vivendum non dedissem. Etenim si summi viri et clarissimi cives Saturnini et   273

Gracchorum et Flacci et superiorum complurium sanguine non modo se non   274

contaminarunt sed etiam honestarunt, certe verendum mihi non erat ne quid   275

hoc parricida civium interfecto invidiae mihi in posteritatem redundaret. Quod   276

si ea mihi maxime impenderet, tamen hoc animo fui semper ut invidiam virtute   277

partam gloriam, non invidiam putarem.   278

273-74 **Saturnini ... Flacci**: Saturninus, an advocate of the **plebs**, was assassinated in 100 B.C. The
Gracchi and Flaccus, that is, Marcus Fulvius Flaccus, are the same as the ones mentioned by
Cicero in 28-34.

275-76 **ne quid ... invidiae**: "Any ill will." **Invidiae** is a partitive genitive with **quid**.

276   **hoc parricida ... interfecto**: **Hoc parricida** = Catiline. An ablative absolute equivalent to a
conditional, i.e., **si hic parricida interfectus esset**.
    mihi: Dative governed by **redundaret**.
    Quod: "But."

277   **ea**: = **invidia**.

277-78 **ut ... gloriam ... putarem**: Cicero says that unpopularity, **invidia**, brought about by strength
of character, **virtus**, is really not unpopularity at all, but rather glory.
    gloriam: A predicate accusative. Translate as if the word order were: **invidiam virtute
partam esse gloriam, non invidiam.**

adultus/a/um full-grown, mature

aggrego *1* to collect

alo -ere -ui altum to support

animadverto -ere -verti -versum to punish

comprimo -ere -pressi -pressum to suppress

consulatus -us *m.* consulship

corroboro *1* to strengthen, encourage

crudeliter *adv.* cruelly

dissimulo *1* to cover up, conceal

eicio -ere -ieci -iectum to drive away; banish

eodem *adv.* in the same place

erumpo -ere -rupi -ruptum to break out, rush out

exstinguo -ere -stinxi -stinctum to destroy, annihilate

fateor -eri fassus sum to admit, acknowledge

fortasse *adv.* perhaps

immineo -ere *def. v. w/ dat.* to overhang; threaten

imperitus/a/um inexperienced

insidiae -arum *f. pl.* ambush; trap, plot

intendo -ere -tendi -tentum to intend; go

latrocinium -i *n.* band of robbers

maturitas -atis *f.* ripeness, maturity

mollis -e soft, weak

nascor nasci natus sum to grow, arise

naufragus -i *m.* survivor; a bankrupt

nescio -ire -ivi -itum to be ignorant, not know

paulisper *adv.* for a little while

penitus *adv.* deep, deeply

pestis -is *f.* plague; destruction

quo pacto how

regie *adv.* in the manner of a king, despotically

relevo *1* to relieve, ease

reprimo -ere -pressi -pressum to restrain, confine

resideo -ere -sedi to stay behind, be left

semen -inis *n.* seed; origin

stirps -is *f.* stem; source

tollo -ere sustuli sublatum to destroy, wipe out

undique *adv.* from everywhere, on all sides

vena -ae *f.* vein, artery

versor *1* to live, dwell

vetus veteris long-established, old

---

279   **Quamquam**: "And yet." Corrective (cf. 211).
       non nulli: "Some" (**litotes**).
       hoc ordine: = The Senate.

280   **qui**: The antecedent is **non nulli** in 279.

281   **aluerunt ... corroboraverunt**: "Have nourished ... have strengthened."

281-82 **quorum auctoritate**: "And on the strength of their authority" (cf. 205 and note). **Quorum** is a coordinating relative; the antecedent is **non nulli** in 279.

283   **factum esse**: The subject of the infinitive in translation is "it," i.e., the execution of Catiline.

284   **Manliana castra**: "Manlius's camp" (cf. 98). Catiline did go to this camp. See *Catiline and Conspiracy*, page xi.

[30] Quamquam non nulli sunt in hoc ordine qui aut ea quae imminent non   279
videant aut ea quae vident dissimulent; qui spem Catilinae mollibus sententiis   280
aluerunt coniurationemque nascentem non credendo corroboraverunt; quorum   281
auctoritate multi non solum improbi verum etiam imperiti, si in hunc   282
animadvertissem, crudeliter et regie factum esse dicerent.   283

Nunc intellego, si iste, quo intendit, in Manliana castra pervenerit, neminem   284
tam stultum fore qui non videat coniurationem esse factam, neminem tam   285
improbum qui non fateatur. Hoc autem uno interfecto intellego hanc rei publicae   286
pestem paulisper reprimi, non in perpetuum comprimi posse.   Quod si sese   287
eiecerit secumque suos eduxerit et eodem ceteros undique collectos naufragos   288
aggregarit, exstinguetur atque delebitur non modo haec tam adulta rei publicae   289
pestis verum etiam stirps ac semen malorum omnium.   290
[XIII] [31] Etenim iam diu, patres conscripti, in his periculis coniurationis insidiisque   291
versamur, sed nescio quo pacto omnium scelerum ac veteris furoris et audaciae   292
maturitas in nostri consulatus tempus erupit.   Hoc si ex tanto latrocinio iste   293
unus tolletur, videbimur fortasse ad breve quoddam tempus cura et metu   294
esse relevati, periculum autem residebit et erit inclusum penitus in venis   295

285-86 **qui ... videat ... qui ... fateatur**: Relative clauses of result.

286-87 **Hoc ... posse**: Note the **alliteration** and the **antithesis** of the infinitives **reprimi** and **comprimi**.

289   **aggregarit**: = **aggregaverit** (**syncopation**).

292   **nescio quo pacto**: "Somehow." The **quo pacto** literally introduces an indirect question after the main verb **nescio**, but the Romans used the phrase often enough that the feeling of a question had been completely lost. Thus the verb **erupit** (293) is indicative.

293   **in ... tempus**: The accusative after **in**, when taken closely with **maturitas** and **erupit**, seems to suggest that the conspiracy was destined to break out during Cicero's consulship.

aeger/gra/grum sick

aestus -us *m.* heat, glow

afflicto *1* to distress, torment

bibo -ere bibi bibitum to drink

comparo *1* to collect

congrego *1* to assemble

consensio -onis *f.* agreement, unanimity

curia -ae *f.* the Senate house

desino -ere -sii -situm to cease, stop

diligentia -ae *f.* attention, energy

fax -cis *f.* torch, firebrand

febris -is *f.* fever

frons -tis *f.* forehead

gelidus/a/um very cold, icy

iacto *1* to throw, hurl

illustro *1* to make clear

inflammo *1* to set on fire

ingravesco -ere *def. v.* to worsen, become aggravated

inscribo -ere -scripsi -scriptum to write upon

insidior *1 w/ dat.* to lie in wait for, plot against

malleolus -i *m.* small hammer; firebrand

morbus -i *m.* disease

murus -i *m.* wall (of a city)

obsideo -ere -sedi -sessum *w/ dat.* to besiege; lie in wait for

opprimo -ere -pressi -pressum to crush

patefacio -ere -feci -factum to lay open; disclose

primo *adv.* at first, in the beginning

profectio -onis *f.* departure, a setting out

qua re and for this reason, therefore

secedo -ere -cessi -cessum to withdraw, go away

secerno -ere -crevi -cretum to separate, set apart

tribunal -alis *n.* platform

urbanus/a/um of the city, urban

vena -ae *f.* vein, artery

vindico *1* to punish

viscus -eris *n.* (*usually pl.*) internal organs, vitals

296-99 **Ut ... ingravescet**: Cicero uses an **analogy** to conclude his argument.

297 **febrique**: **Febri** is an ablative of a third declension i-stem.

299 **istius**: Catiline.
poena: Ablative of means with **relevatus**.
reliquis vivis: An ablative absolute with conditional force. Translate as if **si reliqui erunt vivi**.

300 **Qua re**: Coordinating relative (cf. 97 and 114).

301 **quod**: "As" (literally, "a thing which"). The antecedent seems to be **muro**, but **murus** is masculine and **quod** must be neuter. Accordingly, Cicero must be referring to the whole situation suggested by the clause **muro ... secernantur**.

atque in visceribus rei publicae. Ut saepe homines aegri morbo gravi, cum aestu   296

febrique iactantur, si aquam gelidam biberunt, primo relevari videntur, deinde   297

multo gravius vehementiusque afflictantur, sic hic morbus qui est in re publica   298

relevatus istius poena vehementius reliquis vivis ingravescet.   299

[32] Qua re secedant improbi, secernant se a bonis, unum in locum congregentur,   300

muro denique, quod saepe iam dixi, secernantur a nobis; desinant insidiari domi   301

suae consuli, circumstare tribunal praetoris urbani, obsidere cum gladiis curiam,   302

malleolos et faces ad inflammandam urbem comparare; sit denique inscriptum   303

in fronte unius cuiusque quid de re publica sentiat. Polliceor hoc vobis, patres   304

conscripti, tantam in nobis consulibus fore diligentiam, tantam in vobis   305

auctoritatem, tantam in equitibus Romanis virtutem, tantam in omnibus bonis   306

consensionem ut Catilinae profectione omnia patefacta, illustrata, oppressa,   307

vindicata esse videatis.   308

---

302   **suae**: = **ipsius**. Emphatic.
consuli: Object of the special verb **insidiari** (301).
circumstare ... curiam: This **tribunal** and the **Curia** were in the **Forum**. Catiline's men had surrounded these places to intimidate those not involved in the conspiracy. In the following lines, Cicero further suggests that an armed attack on the administrative center for Rome's government would be completely foolish.

303   **malleolos**: The ancient equivalent of a Molotov cocktail. In Rome, a **malleolus** was a hollowed-out wooden hammer filled with a loose cloth that had been soaked in sap. The cloth and sap were lit before being thrown.

304   **in fronte**: An allusion to the branding on the forehead of runaway slaves (cf. 124 and note), but here the mark would not necessarily be one of shame.
quid ... sentiat: The indirect question is the subject of **sit ... inscriptum** (303).

304-08 **Polliceor ... videatis**: **Alliteration, anaphora, climax.**

arceo -ere -ui to keep _acc._ away from **ab** _w/ abl._

auspicium -i _n._ sign, omen

constituo -ere -stitui -stitutum to worship

exitium -i _n._ destruction, ruin

foedus -eris _n._ treaty, alliance, contract

impius/a/um irreverent, wicked, shameless

inimicus -i _m._ personal enemy

latro -onis _m._ thief, robber

macto _1_ to afflict, vex

moenia -ium _n. pl._ ramparts, walls of a city

nefarius/a/um unspeakable, wicked

nomino _1_ to name, call

omen -inis _n._ sign, harbinger

parricidium -i _n._ murder, parricide

pernicies -ei _f._ destruction, ruin

pestis -is _f._ pestilence, plague

societas -atis _f._ association

Stator -oris _m._ the Stayer, Preventor (a name give to Jupiter)

supplicium -i _n._ punishment, penalty

---

309   **Hisce**: **-ce** is an intensive suffix added to forms of **hic**, **haec**, **hoc**.
Hisce ominibus: Ablative absolute, or ablative of attendant circumstance, i.e., "with." The omens to which Cicero refers are both the words of his speech and those of the prayer that follows.

309-10 **cum ... cum ... cumque eorum exitio**: "Attended by." Technically these are ablatives of attendant circumstance. By openly going to war, Catiline will serve the "highest welfare of the state." The objects **summa salute** and **exitio** will be caused by Catiline's departure, while the middle two, **peste** and **pernicie**, will figuratively be accompanying Catiline. Note the **chiastic** arrangement.
summa rei publicae salute: "The very existence of the state" (cf. 105 and note).

312-17 **Tu ... mactabis**: Speeches in the Senate often closed with a prayer.

312   **qui isdem quibus ... es constitutus**: Two highly **elliptical** clauses; translate as if they were written **qui es constitutus isdem auspiciis quibus haec urbs constituta est**.
es constitutus: = "began to be worshiped." Note that the antecedent of the relative is found within the relative clause itself.

314   **vita**: "Lives." See note on 113.

315-17 **arcebis ... mactabis**: Cicero's confidence in the outcome is reflected in the future indicative, rather than potential subjunctive.

[33] Hisce ominibus, Catilina, cum summa rei publicae salute, cum tua peste ac   309
pernicie cumque eorum exitio qui se tecum omni scelere parricidioque iunxerunt,   310
proficiscere ad impium bellum ac nefarium.   311

Tu, Iuppiter, qui isdem quibus haec urbs auspiciis a Romulo es constitutus,   312
quem Statorem huius urbis atque imperi vere nominamus, hunc et huius socios   313
a tuis ceterisque templis, a tectis urbis ac moenibus, a vita fortunisque civium   314
omnium arcebis et homines bonorum inimicos, hostes patriae, latrones Italiae   315
scelerum foedere inter se ac nefaria societate coniunctos aeternis suppliciis vivos   316
mortuosque mactabis.   317

Scala/Art Resource, NY

Etruscan Ruins at Faesulae. *Faesulae was the site of Manlius's camp mentioned in lines 42, 98, and 284. After Catiline delivered his rebuttal to Cicero, he did, in fact, leave Rome to join Manlius here.*

49

TABLE OF ABBREVIATIONS

=	same as	inf.	infinitive
<	a form of, from	interr.	interrogative
w/	patterns with	intrans.	intransitive
1	first conjugation	irr.	irregular
abbr.	abbreviation	lit.	literal, literally
abl.	ablative	loc.	locative
acc.	accusative	m.	masculine
act.	active	n.	neuter
adj.	adjective	num.	number, numeral, numerical
adv.	adverb, adverbial	pass.	passive
cf.	compare with	perf.	perfect
comp.	comparative	pers.	person, personal
conj.	conjunction	pl.	plural
dat.	dative	poss.	possessive
def.	defective	prep.	preposition
demon.	demonstrative	pres.	present
dep.	deponent	pron.	pronoun
e.g.	for example	refl.	reflexive
etc.	and the rest	sc.	namely, understand
f.	feminine	sg.	singular
fig.	figurative use	subst.	substantive
fut.	future	superl.	superlative
gen.	genitive	tr.	translate, translation
i.e.	that is	trans.	transitive
impers.	impersonal	v.	verb
indef.	indefinite	voc.	vocative
indecl.	indeclinable		

TABLE OF FIRST NAME ABBREVIATIONS

C.	Gaius	Q.	Quintus
L.	Lucius	Sp.	Spurius
M.	Marcus	T.	Titus
M'.	Manius	Ti.	Tiberius
P.	Publius	V.	Valerius

VOCABULARY

A

a ab abs *prep. w/ abl.* from, away from, by

abeo -ire abii abitum to go away, depart

abhorreo -ere -ui *w/ abl.* to be inconsistent with **ab** w/abl.

absum abesse afui afuturus *irr. v.* to be away, be absent

abutor abuti abusus sum *w/ abl.* to abuse

ac and also (*same as* **atque**)

acer acris acre sharp, harsh, keen; **acrius** *comp. adv.* more harshly, more keenly

acerbus/a/um bitter, severe

acies -ei *f.* sharpness, edge

ad *prep. w/ acc.* to, toward, near, at; *w/ gerund or gerundive for* _verb_ -ing

adduco -ere -duxi -ductum to prompt, induce

adeo *adv.* all the way, right up to; even, in fact

adhibeo -ere -ui -itum to apply, use

adhuc *adv.* up to this point, still

administer -tri *m.* assistant

admiror *1* to wonder at, admire

adulescens -ntis *m./f.* young (man), a youth

adulescentulus -i *m. diminutive* little young man

adultus/a/um full-grown, mature

adventus -us *m.* approach, arrival

aeger/gra/grum sick

aequus/a/um level, even

aestus -us *m.* heat, glow

aeternus/a/um everlasting

affero -ferre attuli allatum to bring to, contribute to

afflicto *1* to distress, torment

aggrego *1* to gather together, collect

agnosco -ere agnovi agnitum to recognize, acknowledge

ago -ere egi actum to lead, drive, do; think; **gratias agere** to give thanks; **agere de aliquo** to carry on about something

Ahala -ae *m.* Ahala

aio ais ait aiunt *def. v.* to say

alienus -i *m.* stranger

aliquando *adv.* at some time, at last

aliquis aliquid *indef. adj./pron.* someone, something; some, any

aliquo *adv.* to somewhere, somewhere

aliquot *indecl. num. adj.* some, several

alius/a/ud other, another; **alius ... alius** one ... another; **alii ... alii** some ... others

alo -ere -ui altum to support

altaria -ium *n. pl.* altar

amentia -ae *f.* madness, folly

amicus/a/um friendly; **amicus -i** *m.* friend, ally

amplissimus/a/um (< **amplus**) *superl. adj.* greatest, most distinguished

amplius (< **amplus**) *comp. adj./adv.* more, greater

amplus/a/um full, large

an *conj.* (*between two questions*) But ...? Or ...? Or is it that ...?

anima -ae *f.* soul, existence

animadverto -ere -verti -versum to direct attention to, notice; punish

animus -i *m.* mind, heart; attention; **animum inducere,** to decide

annus -i *m.* year

ante *prep. w/ acc.* before, in front of

antiquus/a/um old, ancient

aperte *adv.* openly

apud *prep. w/ acc. of person* at the house of

aqua -ae *f.* water

aquila -ae *f.* eagle (and by **synecdoche** the whole legionary standard or pole on which a metal eagle was placed)

arbitror *1* to think, suppose

arceo -ere -ui to keep _acc._ away from **ab** w/ abl.

ardeo -ere arsi arsum to be on fire, burn

argenteus/a/um silver

arma armorum *n. pl.* arms

armatus/a/um armed; **armati** *m. pl. subst.* armed men

aspectus -us *m.* sight, view

assequor -i -secutus sum to accomplish, gain

asservo *1* to watch over, keep under guard

assido -ere -sedi to sit down

at *conj.* but

atque *conj.* and also (*same as* **ac**); **simul atque** *conj.* as soon as

atrox atrocis cruel, inhumane

attendo -ere attendi attentum to pay attention to, listen to

auctor -is *m.* promoter, leader

auctoritas -atis *f.* lead; support, approval; sign

audacia -ae *f.* boldness, recklessness

audeo -ere ausus sum *semi-dep.* to be bold, dare

audio -ire -ivi -itum to hear, listen to

Aurelium *see* **Forum Aurelium**

auris auris *f.* ear

auspicium -i *n.* divination (from birds); sign, omen

aut *conj.* or; **aut ... aut** either ... or

autem *conj.* moreover, however

avus avi *m.* grandfather

B

bacchor *1* revel, rave

bellum -i *n.* war

bibo -ere bibi bibitum to drink

bonus/a/um good; **bona -orum** *n. pl. subst.* goods, property; **boni -orum** *m. pl. subst.* good men

brevis -e brief

C

C. *abbr. for* **Gaius -i** *m.* Gaius

caedes caedis *f.* slaughter, murder

caelum -i *n.* sky

calamitas -atis *f.* calamity, ruin

campus -i *m.* plain, marching field

capio capere cepi captum to seize

carcer -eris *m.* cell, prison

careo -ere -ui *w/ abl.* to need; be without, go without

carus/a/um dear

castra -orum *n. pl.* camp

casus -us *m.* a falling; chance, mishap, accident

Catilina -ae *m.* Catiline

causa *abl. w/ gen.* for the sake of

causa -ae *f.* cause, reason; case (in court); **de causa** for a reason

cedo cedere cessi cessum *w/ dat.* to yield to, give in to; withdraw from

certus/a/um specific; **certe** *adv.* certainly

ceteri/ae/a the rest, everybody (everything) else

Cicero -onis *m.* Cicero

circumcludo -ere -clusi -clusum to shut in, surround

circumsto -are -steti to surround; threaten

civis -is *m.* citizen

civitas -atis *f.* state

clamo *1* to shout

clarus/a/um bright clear; famous

clemens -ntis merciful, lenient

coepi -isse coeptum *def. v.* began

coërceo -ere -ui -itum to repress

coetus -us *m.* meeting, gathering

cogito *1* to think

cognosco -ere -novi -nitum to learn; *perf.* know

collectus/a/um gathered

colloco *1* to station, place

colonia -ae *f.* colony

comes comitis *m./f.* comrade, companion

comitia -orum *n. pl.* election

comitium -i *n.* the Comitium (the meeting place in front of the Senate house)

comitum *gen. pl.* < **comes**

commendatio -onis *f.* recommendation

committo -ere -misi -missum to commit, entrust _acc._ to _dat._

commoveo -ere -movi -motum to move, rouse

communis -e common

comparo *1* to join, collect; compare

comperio -ire -peri -pertum to find out, discover, learn

competitor -is *m.* rival, opponent

complures compluria (complura) several, many

comprehendo -ere -prehendi -prehensum to seize, arrest

comprimo -ere -pressi -pressum to repress, suppress

conatus -us *m.* attempt, undertaking

concedo -ere -cessi -cessum to retire; submit

concito *1* to excite, stir up, incite

concupisco -ere -cupivi -cupitum to long for, desire

concursus -us *m.* gathering

condemno *1 w/ gen.* to find _acc._ guilty of _gen._

confero conferre contuli collatum to bring together, assign; **conferre se** to betake oneself, go

confestim *adv.* immediately

conficio -ere -feci -fectum to complete, finish; weaken, destroy

confido -ere -fisus sum *semi-dep.* to trust, be confident

confirmo *1* to strengthen; assert

conflagro *1* to burn up, be consumed

conflo *1* to blow together, throw together; **invidiam conflare**, to arouse animosity towards _dat._

congrego *1* to assemble, gather together

conicio -ere -ieci -iectum to throw together, hurl

coniungo -ere -iunxi -iunctum to join together

coniurati -orum *m. pl.* conspirators

coniuratio -onis *f.* conspiracy

conor -ari -atus sum to try, attempt

conscientia -ae *f.* common knowledge

conscribo -ere -scripsi -scriptum to enroll, enlist; *in the phrase* **patres conscripti** *voc. pl.* conscript fathers, senators

consensio -onis *f.* agreement, unanimity

conservo *1* to save

consilium -i *n.* advice, plan of action; debate; **consilium capere** to adopt a plan

conspicio -ere -spexi -spectum to get sight of, look at

constituo -ere -stitui -stitutum to decide (upon), designate; establish; *fig.* worship

constringo -ere -strinxi -strictum to tie up, bind, choke off

consul -is *m.* consul

consularis -e of consular rank, consular; **comitia consularia** consular elections

consulatus -us *m.* consulship

consulo -ere -sului -sultum to consult

consultum -i *n.* decree

contamino *1* to pollute, stain

contineo -ere -tenui -tentum to restrain, hold in check, contain; **contentus/a/um** content, satisfied

contingo -ere -tigi -tactum *w/ dat.* to affect, happen to

contra *prep. w/ acc.* against

contuli *see* **confero**

contumelia -ae *f.* reproach, insult

convenio -ire -veni -ventum to come together; *impers. v.* it is fitting, proper

convinco -ere -vici -victum to prove wrong, convict
convoco *1* to call together
copia -ae *f. sg.* abundance; *pl.* troops
corpus -oris *n.* body
corrigo -ere -rexi -rectum to correct, fix
corroboro *1* to strengthen, encourage
corruptela -ae *f.* corruption, temptation
cotidie *adv.* every day
credo -ere -idi -itum *w/ dat.* to believe, trust
cresco -ere crevi cretum to grow, increase
crudeliter *adv.* cruelly; **crudelius** *comp. adv.* too cruelly
cum *prep. w/ abl.* with, along with
cum *conj.* when, since, although
cumulo *1* to heap up, increase
cunctus/a/um all, the whole
cupiditas -atis *f.* desire
cupio -ere -ivi -itum to desire
cura -ae *f.* concern, anxiety
curia -ae *f.* the Senate house
custodia -ae *f.* guard, arrest
custodio -ire -ivi -itum to guard, watch over
custos custodis *m./f.* guardian

D

de *prep. w/ abl.* from, about, concerning
debeo -ere -ui -itum to owe, ought
decerno -ere -crevi -cretum to decide, vote, decree
declinatio -onis *f.* a bending; sidestep
dedecus -oris *n.* disgrace
defendo -ere -fendi -fensum to defend, ward off
deficio -ere -feci -fectum to fall short; abandon, defect
defigo -ere -fixi -fixum to fasten, fix; drive, plunge
deinde *adv.* next, second
delecto *1* to please, delight
deleo -ere -evi -etum to destroy
deligo -ere -legi -lectum to choose, select, pick
demigro *1* to depart, leave
denique *adv.* finally, in short
depono -ere -posui -positum to set down; put aside
deprecor *1* to pray to avert; plead against
derelinquo -ere -liqui -lictum to abandon
desidero *1* to long for, miss, desire
designo *1* to point out, elect
desino -ere -sii -situm to leave off, cease, stop
desisto -ere -stiti -stitum to stop, cease
desum deesse defui *irr. v. w/ dat.* to lack; fail
detestor *1* to curse, denounce; avert
detrimentum -i *n.* harm; **detrimentum capere** to receive harm
deus -i *m.* god; **di** *voc./nom. pl.*
devoveo -ere -vovi -votum to devote, consecrate

dexter/tra/trum right; **dextra** *and* **dextera -ae** *f. subst.* right hand
dico -ere dixi dictum to say, claim
dies -ei *m.* (*or f. for special days*) day
difficultas -atis *f.* trouble, difficulty
dignus/a/um *w/ abl.* worthy of
diligens -ntis careful, attentive; **diligenter** *adv.* carefully
diligentia -ae *f.* attention, energy
dimitto -ere -misi -missum to let out, dismiss
direptio -onis *f.* plundering, pillaging
discedo -ere -cessi -cessum to depart, leave
discessus -us *m.* departure, withdrawal
disciplina -ae *f.* training, instruction
discribo -ere -scripsi -scriptum to write down, describe
dissimulo *1* to cover up, conceal
dissolutus/a/um irresponsible
distribuo -ere -tribui -tributum to divide, assign
diu *adv.* for a long time; **diutius** *comp. adv.* longer
do dare dedi datum to give
dolor -is *m.* pain, suffering
domesticus/a/um of the household, familial
domus -us *f.* house; **domi** *loc.* at home
dubito *1* to hesitate
duco -ere duxi ductum to lead, drive
dudum *adv.* some time, for a long time
duint *archaic pres. subjunctive of* **do -are**
dum *conj.* while, until; **dum modo** so long as, provided that
duo duae duo two
dux ducis *m.* leader

E

ecquis ecquid anyone, anything; any _noun_ at all
educo -ere -duxi -ductum to lead out, lead away
effero efferre extuli elatum to bring out, remove; lift up, raise
effrenatus/a/um unbridled, unrestrained
effugio -ere -fugi -fugitum to escape, avoid
egi *see* **ago**
ego mei *pers. pron.* I, me
egredior -i -gressus sum to go out, leave, depart
eicio -ere -ieci -iectum to throw out, drive away; banish
elabor -i -lapsus sum to slip away, escape
eludo -ere -lusi -lusum to play at, mock
emitto -ere -misi -missum to send out, let out
emorior -i -mortuus sum to die off, die
enim *conj.* for, indeed, in fact
eo ire ivi (ii) itum to go
eodem *adv.* in the same place
eques equitis *m.* knight, member of the equestrian order
eripio -ere -ripui -reptum to snatch away

erumpo -ere -rupi -ruptum to break out, rush out

et *conj.* and, also; **et ... et** both ... and

etenim *conj.* and indeed, and really

etiam *adv.* still, also, even

Etruria -ae *f.* Etruria (the district northwest of Rome)

everto -ere -verti -versum to overthrow, ruin

evocator -is *m.* recruiter

ex *prep. w/ abl.* from, out of, away from

exaudio -ire -audivi -auditum to hear clearly, perceive

excido -ere -cidi to fall out, fall

excludo -ere -clusi -clusum to shut out

exeo -ire -ii -itum to go out, leave

exerceo -ere -ercui -ercitum *trans. v.* to practice, train

exhaurio -ire -hausi -haustum to drain off, drink down

existimo *1* to estimate, judge, appraise

exitium -i *n.* destruction, ruin

exorior -iri -ortus sum to arise; begin, be produced

exsilium -i *n.* exile

exsisto -ere exstiti exstitum to come forth, appear; exist

exspecto *1* to wait for, await, expect

exstinguo -ere -stinxi -stinctum to quench; destroy, annihilate

exsul -is *m./f.* exile

exsulto *1, w/ dat.* to leap up; revel in, delight in

extorqueo -ere -torsi -tortum to wrest away, take by force

extra *prep. w/ acc.* outside of

extulit *see* **effero**

F

facilis -e easy, simple

facinus -oris *n.* deed; crime, outrage

facio -ere feci factum to do, make, act; **factu** *supine* "to do"

factum -i *n.* deed

falcarii -orum *m. pl.* Scythemakers' Street (a neighborhood in Rome)

fallo -ere fefelli falsum to deceive, disappoint, trick

fama -ae *f.* reputation

fames -is *f.* hunger, starvation; want, famine

fateor -eri fassus sum to admit, confess; claim

fauces faucium *f. pl.* throat, jaws; pass (of a mountain)

fax facis *f.* torch, firebrand

febris -is *f.* fever

fefelli *see* **fallo**

fero ferre tuli latum to bear; receive, get; tolerate; say

ferrum -i *n.* iron; *fig.* sword

finis -is *m.* end, limit

fio fieri factus sum *irr. v.* to be made, become, happen

firmo *1* to strengthen

firmus/a/um strong, secure, reliable

Flaccus -i *m.* Flaccus

flagitium -i *n.* deed of shame, outrage, disgrace

foedus -eris *n.* treaty, alliance; contract

fore *alternative form of* **futurum esse**

fortasse *adv.* perhaps

fortis -e strong, brave

fortitudo -inis *f.* bravery, strength, courage

fortuna -ae *f.* luck; **Fortuna -ae** *f.* the goddess Fortune; **fortunae -arum** *f. pl.* possessions, property

forum -i *n.* marketplace; the Roman forum

Forum Aurelium -i *n.* Forum Aurelium (a small market town in Etruria about 75 miles north of Rome on the Via Aurelia)

frango -ere fregi fractum to break, destroy

frequentia -ae *f.* crowd

frigus -oris *n.* cold, chill

frons -ntis *f.* forehead; appearance

fuga -ae *f.* flight, escape

Fulvius -i *m.* Fulvius

funestus/a/um deadly, fatal; mournful

furiosus/a/um mad, raving, insane

furor furoris *m.* madness, insanity

G

gaudium -i *n.* gladness, delight, enjoyment

gelidus/a/um very cold, icy

gens -ntis *f.* family, race, clan

gladiator -is *m.* gladiator; thug, ruffian

gladius -i *m.* sword

gloria -ae *f.* glory

Gracchi -orum *m. pl.* the Gracchi brothers

Gracchus -i *m.* Gracchus

gradus -us *m.* step; **gradus honorum** the sequence of offices

gratia -ae *f.* favor, thanks; **gratiam habere** to give thanks; **gratiam referre** to return a favor

gravis -e weighty, serious; **graviter** *adv.* seriously; **gravius** more seriously

H

habeo -ere -ui -itum to have, hold

habito *1* to inhabit, live (in a place)

haereo -ere haesi haesum to stick to, cling to

hebesco -ere *def. v.* to grow dull

hic *adv.* here

hic haec hoc *demonstrative pron./adj.* this; *pl.* these

hisce *dat./abl. intensive of* **hic haec hoc**

homo hominis *m.* man, person; *pl.* people

honesto *1* to dignify, honor, adorn

honestus/a/um noble, worthy, honorable

honor -oris *m.* honor, office; **cursus honorum** the sequence of offices

hora -ae *f.* hour, time

horribilis -e horrible

hortor *1* to urge, encourage

hostis hostis *m./f.* enemy (of the state)

humus -i *f.* ground, soil, earth; **humi** *loc.* on the ground

I

iaceo -ere iacui *intrans. v.* to lie, recline

iacto *1* to throw about, hurl, brandish; **se iactare** to brag, boast

iam *adv. w/ present tense* now, right now; *w/ past tense* already; *w/ future tense* presently, soon; **iam diu** for a long time now; **iam nemo** no longer anyone; **iam pridem** long ago

Ianuarius/a/um of January

idem (isdem) eadem idem *demonstrative adj./pron.* the same; likewise, also; **idem** *adv.* likewise, similarly

Idus Iduum *f. pl.* the Ides (the 15th of March, May, July, and October; the 13th of other months)

igitur *conj.* therefore

ignominia -ae *f.* shame, dishonor

ignoro *1* to be unaware of; fail to recognize

ille illa illud *demon. pron.* that; *pl.* those

illecebra -ae *f.* enticement, charm

illustro *1* to reveal, disclose

immanitas -atis *f.* enormity, ferocity

immineo -ere *def. v. w/ dat.* to overhang; threaten

immitto -ere -misi -missum to send in, send against

immo *adv.* no, rather

immortalis -e immortal, undying

impedio -pedire -pedivi -peditum to hinder, prevent

impendeo -ere *def. v. w/ dat.* to overhang, threaten

imperator -oris *m.* commander, general

imperitus/a/um inexperienced

imperium -i *n.* command, power

impero *1* to command

impetro *1* to obtain; prevail

impetus -us *m.* attack

impius/a/um undutiful, irreverent; wicked, shameless

importunus/a/um grievous, dangerous, cruel, savage

improbus/a/um wicked, base, shameless

impunitus/a/um unpunished, unchecked

in *prep. w/ acc.* into, to; *w/ acc. of person* against; *w/ abl.* in, on, among

inanis -e empty

incendium -i *n.* fire; *pl.* arson

includo -ere -clusi -clusum to shut in, shut up, enclose

incredibilis -e unbelievable

increpo -are -crepui -crepitum to rattle, sound, make a noise

induco -ere -duxi -ductum to bring; persuade; **animum inducere** to decide

ineo -ire -ii -itum to enter into; to attempt

inertia -ae *f.* laziness, neglect

infero -ferre intuli illatum to bring <u>acc.</u> against <u>dat.</u> ; **bellum inferre** to wage war on <u>dat.</u>

infestus/a/um hostile, dangerous

infitior *1* to deny, contradict

inflammo *1* to set on fire; inflame, excite

ingravesco -ere *def. v.* to worsen, become aggravated

inimicus -i *m.* personal enemy

initio *1* to initiate, consecrate

iniuria -ae *f.* harm, injustice; **iniuria** *abl. sg.* wrongly, unjustly

inopia -ae *f.* need, poverty

inquam inquis inquit *def. v.* to say

inscribo -ere -scripsi -scriptum to write upon, assign, mark

insidiae -arum *f. pl.* ambush; trap, plot

insidior *1 w/ dat.* to lie in wait for, plot against

intellego -ere -lexi -lectum to understand

intendo -ere -tendi -tentum to stretch, extend; aim at, intend; go

inter *prep. w/ acc.* between, among

intercedo -ere -cessi -cessum to pass, occur

interficio -ere -feci -fectum to kill, murder

interitus -us *m.* ruin, death, destruction

interrogo *1* to ask

intersum -esse -fui -futurus to be between

intestinus/a/um internal

intra *prep. w/ acc.* inside

inuro -ere -ussi -ustum *w/ dat.* to burn into, brand upon

invenio -ire -veni -ventum to come upon, find

invidia -ae *f.* envy, ill will; unpopularity; **invidiam conflare** to arouse animosity towards <u>dat.</u>

invito *1* to invite, ask; attract, allure

ipse ipsa ipsum *intensive pron.* himself, herself, itself; the very <u>noun</u>

irretio -ire -retivi -retitum to catch in a net, ensnare, entangle

is ea id *demon. pron.* he, she, it

isdem *see* **idem**

isse *perf. inf. of* **eo ire**

iste ista istud *demon. pron.* that of yours; *pejorative* this here

ita *adv.* so, in this way; *followed by a quotation* as follows

Italia -ae *f.* Italy

iubeo iubere iussi iussum to order

iucundus/a/um pleasant

iudicium -i *n.* judgment, sentence, conviction

iudico *1* to decide, judge, declare

iungo -ere iunxi iunctum to join (together)

Iuppiter Iovis *m.* Jupiter

ius iuris *n.* right, justice, law; **iure** *abl. sg.* rightly, justly

iussus -us *m.* command, order; **iussu** *abl. sg.* by order, at the command

iustus/a/um right, just, appropriate

K

Kal. *see* **Kalendae**
Kalendae -arum *f. pl.* the Kalends, the first of the month

L

L. *abbr. for* **Lucius -i** *m.* Lucius
labefacto *1* to shake, weaken, destroy
labor -is *m.* labor; hardship
Laeca -ae *m.* Laeca
laetitia -ae *f.* joy, delight
latro -onis *m.* thief, robber
latrocinium -i *n.* robbery, piracy; band of robbers
laus laudis *f.* praise
lectus -i *m.* bed, couch
lenis -e soft, smooth, mild, gentle
Lepidus -i *m.* Lepidus
lex legis *f.* law; **legem rogare** to pass into law
liber/bera/berum free; **liberi -orum** *m. pl. subst.* children
libero *1* to free <u>acc.</u> from <u>abl.</u>
libido -inis *f.* desire, passion
licet licere licuit *impers. v.* it is permitted
locus -i *m.* place
longe *adv.* far, by far
loquor -i locutus sum to speak
lux lucis *f.* light; dawn

M

M. *abbr. for* **Marcus -i** *m.* Marcus
M'. *abbr. for* **Manius -i** *m.* Manius
machinor *1* to devise, plan
macto *1* to glorify; sacrifice; afflict, vex; kill
Maelius -i *m.* Maelius
magis *adv.* more, rather
magnus/a/um great
maior maioris (< **magnus**) *irr. comp.* greater, larger; **maiores -um** *m. pl. subst.* ancestors; **mos maiorum** tradition of the ancestors, customs
malleolus -i *m.* small hammer; firebrand
malo malle malui *irr. v.* to prefer
malus/a/um bad
mando *1* to hand over, entrust; order, command
mane *adv.* early in the morning
Manlianus/a/um of Manlius
Manlius -i *m.* Manlius
manus -us *f.* hand; band, gang
Marcellus -i *m.* Marcellus
maritus -i *m.* husband
Marius -i *m.* Marius
mature *adv.* promptly, at the right time

maturitas -atis *f.* ripeness, maturity
mavis *2nd pers. sg. of* **malo**
maximus/a/um (< **magnus**)*irr. superl.* greatest; **maxime** *adv.* most
mediocriter *adv.* moderately, fairly, not very much
meditor *1* to contemplate, consider; plan, devise
mehercule (me hercule) *interjection* by Hercules!
memini meminisse *def. v. w/ gen.* to remember
memoria -ae *f.* memory; **post memoriam** within memory
mens mentis *f.* mind; disposition
Metellus -i *m.* Metellus
metuo -ere metui to fear, be afraid of
metus -us *m.* fear, dread, anxiety
meus/a/um my, mine
minus *comp. adv.* less, fewer; not
misericordia -ae *f.* compassion, mercy, pity
mitto -ere misi missum to send
modus -i *m.* type, manner; (**dum**) **modo** so long as, provided that; **eius modi** of this type; **non modo ... sed etiam** not only ... but also
moenia -ium *n. pl.* ramparts, walls of a city, defenses
moles -is *f.* mass, weight, burden
molior -iri molitus sum to try, attempt
mollis -e soft, tender, weak
mora -ae *f.* delay
morbus -i *m.* sickness, disease
mors mortis *f.* death
mortuus/a/um dead
mos moris *m.* habit, custom; *pl.* character, practice; **mos maiorum** tradition of the ancestors, customs
moveo -ere movi motum to move; affect
multo *1* to punish
multus/a/um much; *pl.* many; **multo** *adv.* far, by far, much
munio -ire -ivi -itum to fortify, protect
murus -i *m.* wall (of a city)
muto *1* to change

N

nam *conj.* for
nanciscor -i nactus sum to obtain, secure, receive
nascor nasci natus sum to be born; arise, grow
natura -ae *f.* nature
naufragus -i *m.* castaway, survivor; a bankrupt
ne *conj.* no, not; that ... not; lest; **ne ... quidem** not even
-ne *interr. enclitic introducing a question; in indirect questions* whether
nec *conj.* and ... not; **nec ... nec** neither ... nor (*same as* **neque**)
necessarius -i *m.* relative, client
necesse *indecl. adj.* necessary (*in constructions with* **esse** *and* **habere**)

nefarius/a/um unspeakable, wicked

neglego -ere -lexi -lectum to disregard, neglect

nego *1* to say ... not; deny

nemo neminis *m./f.* no one; **iam nemo** no longer anyone

neque *conj.* and ... not; **neque ... neque** neither ... nor (*same as* **nec**)

nequitia -ae *f.* worthlessness, badness

nescio -ire -ivi -itum to be ignorant, not know

nex necis *f.* murder, slaughter, death

nihil *indecl. noun* nothing; *adv.* in no way at all

nimis *adv.* too, too much

nimium *adv.* too, too much

nisi *conj.* unless, if ... not; except

nocturnus/a/um of the night, nocturnal

nomino *1* to name, call

non *adv.* no, not

nondum *adv.* not yet

nonne *interr. adv.* not; surely ... not

nos nostrum/nostri we, us

noster/tra/trum our

nota -ae *f.* mark, sign, brand

noto *1* to mark (down)

November/bris/bre of November

novus/a/um new, strange; **res novae** *f. pl.* revolution

nox noctis *f.* night

nudus/a/um bare

nullus/a/um no, none, no one, nothing

num *interr. adv.* "<u>subject</u> doesn't ..., does <u>subject</u>?", "<u>subject</u> didn't ..., did <u>subject</u>?"; *in an indirect question* whether

numero *1* to count

numerus -i *m.* number

numquam *adv.* never

nunc *adv.* now

nuper *adv.* recently

nuptiae -arum *f. pl.* wedding, marriage

O

O *interjection/direct address* O; *exclamation* Oh

ob *prep. w/ acc.* on account of; **quam ob rem** and for this reason

obeo -ire -ii -itum *w/ dat.* to meet, go up to

obliviscor -i oblitus sum *w/ gen.* to forget

obscuro *1* to cover up, darken

obscurus/a/um concealed, concealed, obscure; **obscure** *adv.* obscurely

obsideo -ere -sedi -sessum (*sometimes w/ dat.*) to besiege, surround; lie in wait for

obsisto -ere obstiti obstitum *w/ dat.* to resist, thwart

obtempero *1* to comply with, obey, submit

occido -ere -cidi -cisum to kill, murder

occupo *1* to occupy, seize

oculus -i *m.* eye

odi odisse *def. v. in perf. tenses only* to hate

odium -i *n.* hate, grudge

offensus/a/um disliked, offensive

omen -inis *n.* sign, token, harbinger

omitto -ere -misi -missum to leave out, disregard

omnis -e *sg.* every, each; *pl.* all

Opimius -i *m.* Opimius

opinor *1* to suppose

oportet oportere oportuit *impers. v. in pres. tense* it is right, ought; *in past tenses* ought to have <u>inf.</u> -ed (*see note on 16*)

opprimo -ere -pressi -pressum to oppress; suppress, crush

optimates -ium *m. pl.* the optimates, the aristocratic party

optimus/a/um *superl. of* **bonus** best

oratio -onis *f.* speech; **orationem habere** to give a speech

orbis orbis *m.* circle, globe; **orbis terrae** the world

ordo ordinis *m.* rank, class, order, body

os oris *n.* mouth, face, expression

ostento *1* to show, exhibit; show off, display, boast

otiosus/a/um at leisure, idle; **otiosi** *m. pl. subst.* the neutral ones, the idle

otium -i *n.* leisure

P

P. *abbr. for* **Publius -i** *m.* Publius

pactum -i *n.* agreement, bargain; manner, way; **pacto** *abl. sg.* in a way; **quo pacto** how

Palatium -i *n.* the Palatine (the hill immediately south of the **Forum**)

pango -ere pepigi pactum to arrange, agree upon; dedicate, grant

parens -ntis *m./f.* parent

paries parietis *m.* wall (of a house)

pario -ere peperi partum to bring forth, produce; acquire, get

paro *1* to prepare, provide

parricida -ae *m.* assassin, parricide

parricidium -i *n.* murder, parricide

pars partis *f.* part; side

particeps -cipis *m. w/ gen.* participant in

partus/a/um *see* **pario**

parvus/a/um small

patefacio -ere -feci -factum to make open, lay open; disclose

pateo -ere patui to lie out in the open, be open

pater patris *m.* father

patientia -ae *f.* patience, endurance

patior -i passus sum to bear, endure; allow

patres conscripti *voc. pl.* senators

patria -ae *f.* fatherland, country

paucus/a/um few

paulisper *adv.* for a little while

paulo *adv.* a little; **paulo ante** a little while ago, shortly before

paulum -i *n.* a little bit

penitus *adv.* deep, deeply

peperit *see* **pario**

per *prep. w/ acc.* through, across; by

percipio -ere -cepi ceptum to seize; observe, learn

perdo -ere -didi -ditum to lose, destroy, corrupt; **perditus/a/um** lost, corrupt, depraved

perfero -ferre -tuli -latum to endure with patience, put up with

perfringo -ere -fregi -fractum to break through/down, violate

perfruor -i -fructus *w/ abl.* to enjoy fully, be greatly delighted with

pergo -ere perrexi perrectum to keep on, proceed, go forward

periclitor *1* to put to the test, risk

periculum -i *n.* danger

permitto -ere -misi -missum to entrust _acc._ to _dat._

permoveo -ere -movi -motum to arouse; prevail upon

pernicies -ei *f.* destruction, disaster, ruin, threat

perniciosus/a/um *w/ dat.* destructive to, ruinous to

perpetuus/a/um continuous, perpetual; **in perpetuum** forever

persaepe *adv.* very often

perspicio -ere -spexi -spectum to see plainly, observe

perterreo -ere -terrui -territum to frighten thoroughly

pertimesco -ere -timui to become alarmed at, fear

pertineo -ere -ui to extend, pertain to, belong to

pervenio -ire -veni -ventum to arrive at

pestis -is *f.* plague, pestilence; destruction

petitio -onis *f.* blow, attack, aim

peto -ere -ivi -itum to fall upon, attack, aim at, seek

placet placere placuit *impers. v.* it is pleasing

placo *1* to soothe, appease

plane *adv.* openly

plebs plebis *f.* common people, plebians

plurimus/a/um (< **multus**) *superl. adj.* most, very many

poena -ae *f.* penalty, punishment; **poena rei publicae** death penalty

polliceor -eri pollicitus sum to promise

pontifex pontificis *m.* priest; **pontifex maximus** chief priest

populus -i *m.* people

porta -ae *f.* gate

possum posse potui *irr. v.* to be able

post *prep. w/ acc.* after, behind; **post memoriam** within memory

postea *adv.* later on, afterwards

posteritas -atis *f.* the future; future generations

postulo *1* to demand, ask, beg, request

potius *comp. adv.* rather; **potius ... quam** *conj.* rather than

praeclarus/a/um distinguished, famous

praedico *1* to announce, claim

praedico -ere -dixi -dictum to foretell, predict

praefero -ferre -tuli -latum to carry _acc._ before/in front of _dat._

praemitto -ere -misi -missum to send forward, dispatch in advance

Praeneste -is *n.* Praeneste (a town twenty miles east of Rome)

praesens -entis present, at hand

praesentia -ae *f.* presence

praesidium -i *n.* defense, guard, garrison; escort

praestolor *1* *w/ dat.* to wait for, expect

praetereo -ire -ivi (-ii) -itum to pass over, forego

praetermitto -ere -misi -missum to pass over, leave out

praetor -is *m.* praetor

praetuli *see* **praefero**

pridem *adv.* for a long time

pridie *adv.* on the previous day

primus/a/um first; **primo** *adv.* at first, in the beginning; **primum** *adv.* at first, from the beginning

princeps -cipis first, foremost; **principes -um** *m. pl. subst.* leading men, leaders; **principes civitatis** leading citizens

prior prius *comp. adj.* earlier; *of days* before last

privatus/a/um personal; **privatus** *m.* civilian, private citizen

probo *1* to approve, commend, recommend

profectio -onis *f.* departure, a setting out

proficio -ere -feci -fectum to advance, succeed, accomplish; help

proficiscor -i -fectus sum to set out

profugio -ere -fugi to flee, run away, escape

prope *prep. w/ acc.* near

proprius/a/um *w/ gen.* special to, appropriate for

propter *prep. w/ acc.* on account of, because of

prosequor -i -secutus sum to pursue, chase; prosecute; escort

proximus/a/um nearest, next; last, most recent

publicus/a/um public; **publice** *adv.* publicly; **res publica** *f. sg.* the Republic, commonwealth

pudor -oris *m.* shame, decency

purgo *1* to cleanse, purify

puto *1* to think, suppose

Q

Q. *abbr. for* **Quintus -i** *m.* Quintus

qua re wherefore, and for this reason, therefore

quaeso -ere *def. v.* to beg, ask

quaestio -onis *f.* inquiry, trial, court

quam *conj.* as, than, how; **quam** *w/ adj./adv.* how <u>adj./adv.</u>; *w/ superl.* as <u>adj./adv.</u> as possible; **quam diu** *conj.* as long as; how long; **quam ob rem** therefore

quamquam *conj.* although, and yet

quantus/a/um *interr. adj.* how great

-que *enclitic conj.* and

querimonia -ae *f.* complaint, lament

qui quae quod *relative pron./adj.* who, which, what, that

quia *conj.* since, because

quicquid = quidquid anything

quidam quaedam quoddam (quiddam) *indef. pron./adj.* a certain, some

quidem *adv.* in fact, indeed; **ne ... quidem** not even

quiesco -ere quievi quietum to keep still, take no action

quis quid *interr. pron.* who, what; **quid** *adv.* why; *following* **si, nisi, num,** *and* **ne,** anyone, anything *(same as* **aliquis***)*

quisquam quicquam *indef. pron.* anyone (at all), anything (at all)

quisque quidque *pron. and adj.* each, every

quisquis quidquid *indef. relative pron.* anyone, anything

quo *interr. adv./conj.* (to) where?; **quo pacto** how

quod *conj.* because; the fact that; but

quondam *adv.* at one time, formerly

quoniam *conj.* since

quoque *adv.* too, also

quot *indecl. adj.* how many

quotiens *adv.* how often ...?; *exclamation* how often ...!; *conj.* as often as

quotienscumque *adv.* however often, whenever

R

rapio -ere rapui raptum to seize, snatch, take

ratio -onis *f.* way, manner; reason, thought

recens -entis fresh, recent

recipio -ere -cepi -ceptum to accept, receive; welcome

recognosco -ere -cognovi -cognitum to recall, recount, review

recondo -ere -condidi -conditum to hide, conceal

recta *adv.* straight, directly

redundo *1 w/ dat.* to wash back over; overwhelm

refero -ferre rettuli relatum to bring back; **gratiam referre** to return a favor; **ad senatum referre** to present before the Senate (for debate)

regie *adv.* in the manner of a king, despotically

relevo *1* to lighten; relieve, ease

relinquo -ere -liqui -lictum to abandon, leave behind

reliquus/a/um left over, remaining

remaneo -ere -mansi -mansum to stay behind, remain

remoror *1* to delay, wait on

repello -ere -ppuli -pulsum to drive <u>acc.</u> back from <u>abl.</u>

reperio -ire -pperi -pertum to find, discover

reprimo -ere -pressi -pressum to check, restrain, confine

repudio *1* to reject, refuse

res rei *f.* thing, matter, affair; **res novae** *f. pl.* revolution; **res publica** *f. sg.* the Republic, commonwealth

resideo -ere -sedi to sit down; stay behind, be left

respondeo -ere -spondi -sponsum to respond, answer

responsum -i *n.* answer

revoco *1* to recall, turn away

rogo *1* to ask; *of laws* to pass; **sententiam rogare** to ask the opinion of <u>acc.</u>

Roma -ae *f.* Rome; **Romae** *loc.* at Rome; **Roma** *abl. sg.* from Rome

Romanus/a/um Roman

Romulus -i *m.* Romulus

ruina -ae *f.* downfall, ruin, destruction

S

sacer/cra/crum sacred; **sacra -orum** *n. pl.* rites

sacrarium -i *n.* shrine, sanctuary

saepe *adv.* often; **saepius** *comp. adv.* too often

sagax -acis keen, quick, shrewd

salus -utis *f.* health, safety

saluto *1* to greet, pay respects to; **salutatum** *supine* to greet

sanctus/a/um consecrated, inviolable; pure

sanguis -inis *m.* blood, family; bloodshed, murder

satelles satellitis *m./f.* attendant, accomplice

satis *indecl. subst. and adv.* enough; **satis facere** to satisfy

Saturninus -i *m.* Saturninus

sceleratus/a/um wicked, criminal, vicious; **scelerate** *adv.* criminally

scelus -eris *n.* crime

scientia -ae *f.* knowledge

scio -ire scivi scitum to know

Scipio -onis *m.* Scipio

secedo -ere -cessi -cessum to withdraw, go away

secerno -ere -crevi -cretum to separate, set apart

sed *conj.* but

seditio seditionis *f.* insurrection, rebellion

seiungo -ere -iunxi -iunctum to separate, sever

semen -inis *n.* seed; source, origin

semper *adv.* always

senatus -us *m.* Senate

sensistin = sensisti-ne ...?

sensus -us *m.* feeling, perception

sentventia -ae *f.* thought, opinion; **sententiam rogare** to ask the opinion of _acc._

sentina -ae *f.* bilge water, sewage, dregs

sentio -ire sensi sensum to feel, notice, perceive

sequor -i secutus sum to follow

serus/a/um late; **serius** *comp. adv.* too late

sermo -onis *m.* talk, conversation

Servilius -i *m.* Servilius

servio -ire -ivi -itum *w/ dat.* to serve, labor for

servo *1* to keep, save

servus -i *m.* slave, servant

sese *intensive form of* **sui sibi;** *translate the same as* **se**

Sestius -i *m.* Sestius

severitas -atis *f.* strict action, sternness

si *conj.* if

sic *adv.* thus, in this way

sica -ae *f.* dagger

sicut *conj.* just as

silentium -i *n.* silence

sileo -ere -ui to be quiet, leave unmentioned

similis -e similar, like

simul *adv.* at the same time, at once; **simul atque** *conj.* as soon as

sin *conj.* but if, if on the contrary

sine *prep. w/ abl.* without

singuli/ae/a *distributive pl.* individual, single, each

sino -ere sivi situm to permit, allow

societas -atis *f.* fellowship, association, union

socius -i *m.* ally

sodalis -is *m./f.* companion, friend, pal

soleo -ere -itus sum *semi-dep.* to be accustomed, be used to

solitudo -inis *f.* loneliness; lonely place, wilderness

solus/a/um sole, alone, only; **non solum ... sed etiam** not only ... but also

somnus -i *m.* sleep

Sp. *abbr. for* **Spurius -i** *m.* Spurius

speculor *1* to watch

spes -ei *f.* hope

spiritus -us *m .* breath, breathing, air

sponte (tua) *f. abl. sg. only* of (your) own accord, voluntarily

Stator -oris *m.* the Stayer, Preventor (a name give to Jupiter)

statuo -ere statui statutum to decide

status -us *m.* situation, condition

stirps -is *f.* trunk, stem; source

sto stare steti statum to stand

studeo -ere -ui *w/ dat.* to be eager for, be zealous about

studium -i *n.* eagerness, zeal

stultus/a/um foolish

stuprum -i *n.* defilement; debauchery, lewdness

suadeo -ere suasi suasum *w/ dat. of pers.* advise, urge

subsellium -i *n.* seat, bench, bleacher

sui sibi *refl. pron.* himself, herself, itself; *pl.* themselves

sum esse fui futurus *irr. v.* to be

summus/a/um *superl. adj.* highest, best

superior -ius (< **superus**) *comp. adj.* previous, last; *of days or nights* before last; **superiora -um** *n. pl. subst.* the aforementioned, the foregoing

superus/a/um that above, upper

supplicium -i *n.* punishment, penalty, torture

suscipio -ere -cepi -ceptum to undertake, attempt; submit to, bear

suspectus/a/um suspected

suspicio -onis *f.* suspicion, mistrust

suspicor *1* mistrust, suspect; surmise, suppose

sustineo -ere -tinui -tentum to support; endure, withstand

suus/a/um *refl. adj.* his own, her own, its own; *pl.* their own

T

tabula -ae *f.* tablet; *pl.* (public) records, tables

taceo -ere tacui tacitum to be silent, be quiet

taciturnitas -atis *f.* silence

taeter/tra/trum loathsome, foul, disgusting

tam *adv.* so, so much; **tam ... quam** *conj.* so much ... as

tamen *adv.* still, nevertheless

tametsi *conj.* and yet

tamquam *conj.* just as

tandem *adv.* at length, finally

tantus/a/um so great, such great; **tantum** *adv.* only; **est tanti** it is worth it

tecta -orum *n. pl. lit.* covers, roofs; *fig.* houses, homes

telum -i *n.* weapon, spear, javelin

tempestas -atis *f.* weather, storm

templum -i *n.* temple

tempto *1* to try, attempt

tempus -oris *n.* time; **tempora** *pl.* the times, critical situation

tenebrae -arum *f. pl.* darkness

teneo -ere -ui -tum to keep, hold

terra -ae *f.* land

Ti. *abbr. for* **Tiberius -i** *m.* Tiberius

timeo -ere -ui to fear, be afraid of

timor -oris *m.* fear

tollo -ere sustuli sublatum to lift up, raise; destroy, wipe out

tot *indecl. num. adj.* so many, in such numbers

totiens *adv.* so many times

totus/a/um whole, all

transfero -ferre -tuli -latum to carry <u>acc.</u> across, pass <u>acc.</u> over

transtulisti *see* **transfero**

tribunal -alis *n.* platform

tribunus -i *m.* tribune

trucido *1* to slaughter, butcher

tu tui *pers. pron.* you

tua sponte *see* **sponte**

tuli *see* **fero**

Tullius -i *m.* Tullius

Tullus -i *m.* Tullus

tum *adv.* then, at that time

tumultus -us *m.* riot, insurrection, mutiny; state of emergency

tune = tu-ne

turpitudo -inis *f.* disgrace, shame

tuto *adv.* safely, safe

tuus/a/um *poss. adj.* your

U

ubi *adv.* where; *conj.* when, where

ubinam *adv. in the phrase* **ubinam gentium** where in the world

ullus/a/um any

umquam *adv.* ever

undique *adv.* from everywhere, on all sides

universus/a/um whole, altogether

unus/a/um one, alone; **una** *adv.* together

urbanus/a/um of the city, urban

urbs urbis *f.* city

usque *adv.* all the way

usura -ae *f.* use

ut *conj. w/ subjunctive* in order that, so that, that; *w/ indicative* as, when

uti *conj. same as* **ut**

utilis -e useful, effective, advantageous

utinam *adv.* would that, oh that

uxor -oris *f.* wife

V

V. *abbr. for* **Valerius -i** *m.* Valerius

vacuefacio -ere -feci -factum to make empty, clear, vacate

vagina -ae *f.* sheath, scabbard

valeo -ere valui valitum to be strong, be able; **valere ad** to succeed at

Valerius -i *m.* Valerius

vastitas -atis *f.* devastation, desolation, ruin

vasto *1* to lay waste, destroy

-ve *enclitic conj.* or

vehemens -ntis strong, forceful; **vehementius** *comp. adv.* more strongly, more forcefully

vena -ae *f.* vein, artery

veneror *1* to revere, worship, adore; pay homage to

venio -ire veni ventum to come

vereor -eri veritus sum to fear, be afraid of; respect

vero *adv.* indeed, in fact

versor *1* to be among, be around; live, dwell

verum *conj.* but; **verum etiam** but also

verus/a/um true, well-founded, justifiable; **vere** *adv.* truly

vester/tra/trum your, of yours

vetus -eris long-established, of a former time, old

vexatio -onis *f.* harassing

vexo *1* to frustrate, harass

vicesimus/a/um twentieth

videlicet *adv.* clearly, namely, of course

video -ere vidi visum to see; **videor -eri visus sum** to seem

vigilia -ae *f.* night guard, night watch

vigilo *1* to stay awake; be watchful, be attentive

vilis -e of small price, cheap; poor, mean, base

vinculum -i *n.* fetter, bond, chain

vindico *1* to avenge, punish

vir viri *m.* man

virtus -utis *f.* courage

vis vis *acc. sg.* **vim**, *abl. sg.* **vi**, *f.* strength, force, power

viscus -eris *n. (usually pl.)* internal organs, vitals; bowels, heart

vita -ae *f.* life, lives

vitium -i *n.* fault, crime, vice

vito *1* to avoid, evade

vivo -ere vixi victum to live

vivus/a/um living

vix *adv.* hardly

vixdum *adv.* hardly yet, barely

voco *1* to call

volo velle volui to want, wish

volo *1* fly

voluntas -atis *f.* will, wish, desire

voluptas -atis *f.* pleasure, delight

vox vocis *f.* voice

vulnero *1* to wound, harm; offend

vultus -us *m.* face, expression

BIBLIOGRAPHY

Barnes, E. J. and Ramsey, John T. *Cicero and Sallust: On the Conspiracy of Catiline*. White Plains: Longman, 1988.

Bell, Patricia E. *Imperium et Civitas*. New York: Cambridge University Press, 1988.

Butler, H. E., tr. *Quintilian III: Books VII-IX*. The Loeb Classical Library. Cambridge, MA: Harvard University Press, 1921.

Cape, Robert. "The Rhetoric of Politics in Cicero's *Fourth Catilinarian*." *American Journal of Philology* 116 (1995) 255-277.

Caplan, H., tr. *[Cicero] I: Ad C. Herennium*. The Loeb Classical Library. Cambridge, MA: Harvard University Press, 1954.

Cary, M. And Scullard, H. H. *A History of Rome Down to the Reign of Constantine*. 3rd Edition. London: MacMillan Education Ltd., 1979.

Corbett, Edward P. J. *Classical Rhetoric for the Modern Student*. Oxford: Oxford University Press, 1965.

Craig, Christopher P. "Three Simple Questions for Teaching Cicero's *First Catilinarian*." *Classical Journal* 88 (1993) 255-267.

Gruen, E. S. "Notes on the First Catilinarian Conspiracy." *Classical Philology* 64 (1969) 20-24.

Hayes, J. and Lawall, G., eds. *Teacher's Guide to Cicero*. Amherst: Classical Association of New England, 1995.

Lanham, Richard A. *A Handlist of Rhetorical Terms*. Berkeley: University of California Press, 1991.

MacDonald, C., tr. *Cicero X: In Catilinam I-IV, Pro Murena, Pro Sulla, Pro Flacco*. The Loeb Classical Library. Cambridge, MA: Harvard University Press, 1977.

March, Duane A. "Cicero and the 'Gang of Five'." *Classical World* 82 (1989) 225-234.

May, James M. *Trials of Character: The Eloquence of Ciceronian Ethos*. Chapel Hill and London: University of North Carolina Press, 1988.

Meinecke, Bruno. *Third Year Latin: Revision of Kelsey's Cicero*. Dallas: Allyn and Bacon, Inc., 1962.

Mitchell, Thomas N. *Cicero: The Ascending Years*. New Haven: Yale University Press, 1979.

-----. *Cicero: The Senior Statesman*. New Haven: Yale University Press, 1991.

Moore, Frank G. and Barss, John E. *Orations of Cicero*. Dallas: Ginn and Co., 1929.

Oxford Classical Dictionary. Third Edition. Edited by Simon Hornblower and Antony Spawforth. Oxford: Oxford University Press, 1996.

Phillips, E. J. "Catiline's Conspiracy." *Historia* 25 (1976) 441-448.

Ramsey, John T., ed. *Sallust's Bellum Catilinae*. Atlanta: Scholar's Press, 1984.

Rawson, Elizabeth. *Cicero: A Portrait*. Ithaca, NY: Cornell University Press, 1983.

Scullard, H. H. *From the Gracchi to Nero: A History of Rome from 133 B.C. to A.D. 68*. 5th Edition. New York: Methuen, 1982.

Seager, Robin. "The First Catilinarian Conspiracy." *Historia* 13 (1964) 338-347.

-----. "Iusta Catilinae." *Historia* 22 (1973) 240-248.

Stockton, David, ed. *Thirty-five Letters of Cicero*. Oxford: Oxford University Press, 1969.

Syme, Ronald. *The Roman Revolution*. Oxford: Oxford University Press, 1952.

Ullman, B. L. and Suskin, Albert I. *Latin For Americans: Third Book*. New York: MacMillan, 1983.

Vasaly, Ann. *Representations: Images of the World in Ciceronian Oratory*. Berkeley and Los Angeles: University of California Press, 1993.